BUILDING A
WOOD-FRAMED PANELIZED
YURT

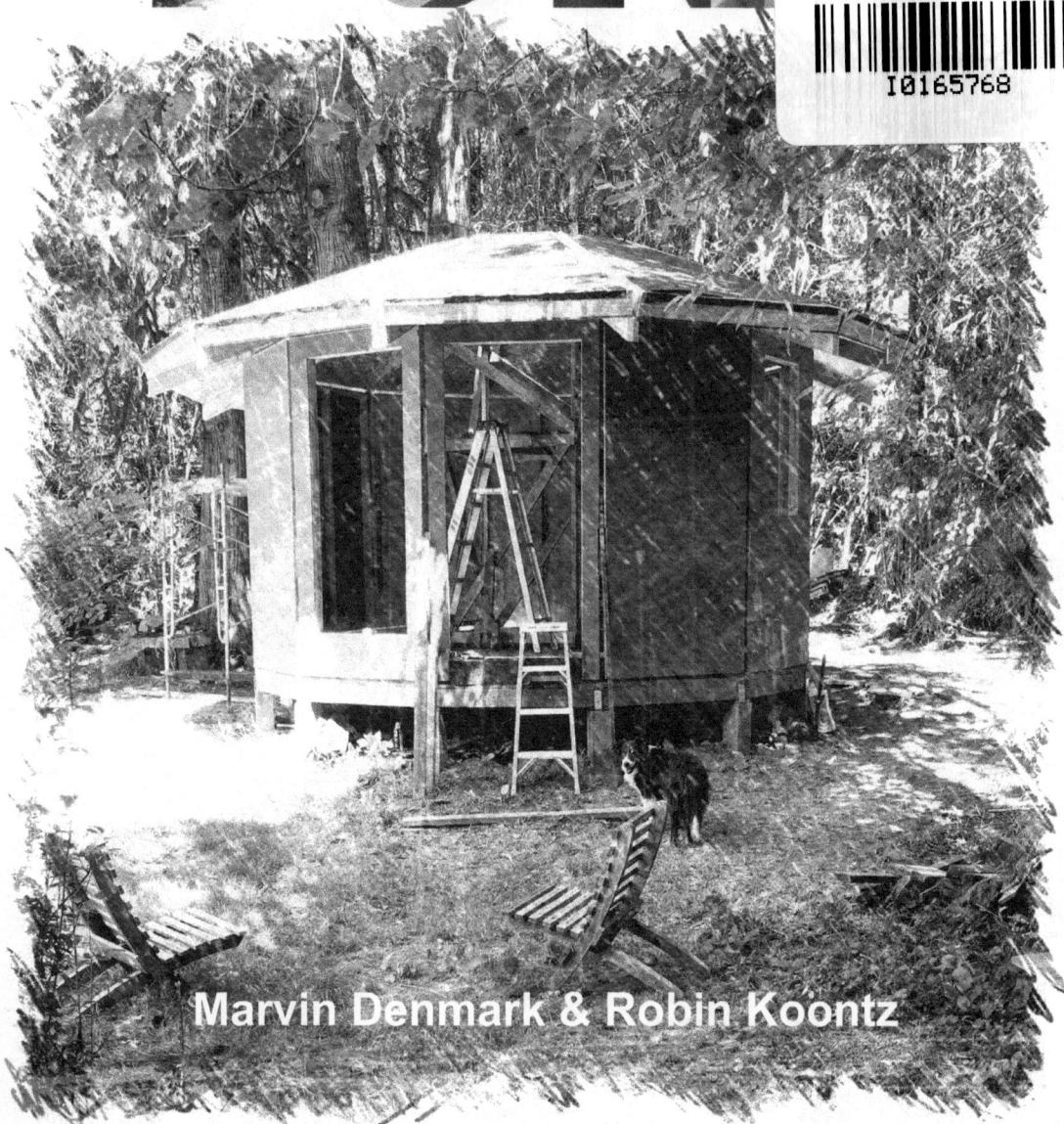

Marvin Denmark & Robin Koontz

YURT

YAKS

YurtYaks
PO Box 336
Noti, OR 97461

10 9 8 7 6 5 4 3 2 1

YurtYaks
ISBN-13: 978-0578408019
ISBN-10: 0578408015

Book design by Robin Koontz
Illustrations by Marvin Denmark
Photographs by the authors except where noted

Color charcoal sketch photo effects courtesy of
CK-FX Photo Studio: www.macphun.com

Library of Congress Cataloging-in-Publication Data
Denmark, Marvin Koontz, Robin
Building a Wood-Framed Panelized Yurt /
Marvin Denmark and Robin Koontz

A Note from the Writer-Editor

This book is not "Yurt Building for Dummies." Some basic skills plus understanding and knowledge of building construction will be required along with a few tools. Common safety practices are important too, including eye and ear protection.

As I was writing and editing our notes and putting together the photos, I watched, questioned, and interviewed Marvin, especially about things that seemed complicated to someone like me with minimal building knowledge and experience. Marvin answered my questions and added more details when I felt they were needed... even when he didn't. He also provided ideas for alternate ways to do things.

Hopefully you will find our book understandable and thorough. There will probably be things that are obvious to you, but you will appreciate the extra explanation on others. We tried to photograph everything, and as you'll see we did not use a studio setting for this project. It's just our messy barn at all hours of the day and during all months of the year.

We hope that our book provides the guidance and information needed in order to build your own wood-framed panelized yurt.

Contents

Introduction

When most people hear the word "yurt," they think of a round structure with animal-skin or canvas walls and a domed roof. But yurts are also constructed using wood panels, and have been for hundreds of years.

While a skin-yurt, with the more modern versions employing canvas or a similar material for the walls and often the roof, is more common, a wooden yurt will hold up better in certain climates and work better for some applications.

When built using modern building techiniques and codes, a yurt can be a sound and permanent structure for a residence or business.

When I built a yurt for the first time, I had been a carpenter and building contractor in western Oregon for about 25 years. A friend recommended me to help a couple that was building a yurt on their property. At the time, there was a local yurt manufacturing company that supplied all the pre-made components. And if you needed it, they would also supply a team to put the yurt up for you. I was hired by the couple to build the foundation and then to see the project through, from the yurt installation along with the team from the yurt company to the finish work. I subsequently consulted on several more yurt jobs for the company.

There are a few companies in the U.S. that offer kits similar to the ones I helped people assemble, and links to some are at the end of this book. But I know there are people like me out there who want to do it themselves, from scratch. So, I decided to build my own yurt at my place, work out all the issues that came up and then share the entire process including photographs and plans. I also published videos that demonstrate some of the steps. Links to those videos are at the end of the book.

Don't get me wrong: building a wood-framed panelized yurt is not easy. The nature of the shape itself forces a builder to truly think outside the box and understand some basic trigonometry. But hopefully the step-by-step instructions and explanations, illustrations, and photos in this book will be all the information anyone who understands basic construction will need to build a solid wood-framed panelized yurt.

What is a Yurt?

The first yurts were constructed and used by nomads in Central Asia. Many yurt dwellers were nomadic herders, managing sheep, goats, or yaks that provided them with food, clothing, and shelter. Three or four times a year, they would pick up and move to the best pastures, depending on the weather and food/water resources. It helped to have a movable shelter, but one that was comfortable and accommodating to their needs for long periods of time, if not their entire lives.

Nomads of the steppe traded with people in the river valleys in order to acquire wood to build their yurts.

Ancient yurts were framed with a wooden lattice that could be collapsed, making it fairly easy to take the structure down and move it to a new location. The top was an open center compression ring that supported the radial rafters. The lattice was tied securely with a rope and coverings were placed over the structure. The cover material was usually fleece from yaks, sheep, or goats that had been worked into wool. They employed a process called felting that fiber artists still use today. The covering might also have been animal hides. The coverings were secured with leather straps or rope. The top piece could be removed if weather allowed for it.

The yurt structure was designed to survive winds and frigid weather. Having no

Wind energy is dispersed around the circular structure of a yurt. The sloping roof is aerodynamic, making it unlikely for winds to tear off the roof beams. The domed roof can also handle heavy snow loads. On the original yurts, many layers of felt and/or hides were used to provide insulation from the harsh cold.

The earliest evidence of yurt dwellings are etchings in Siberia that date to the Bronze Age. Jurt was the Turkic word for their version of a yurt that was later translated in Russia to yurta. Yurts are called gers in Mongolia. Today, more than 75% of Mongolian people live in yurts.

Large yurts were divided up so that family members had their own sections. A stove was in the middle with the chimney going out through the top center. Because the rafters bear the weight of the roof ring, no center pole was necessary.

trees or shrubs to serve as windbreaks, the winds on the steppe can be fierce.

Most yurts today are based on this ancient design, with a number of improvements. They still employ a collapsible frame, radial rafter roof system with a center compression ring and tension cable (not

rope), plus a fabric of some kind, usually canvas, for the roof and walls.

The yurt in this book is also based on the original yurt design, employing a center ring and tension cable, but it is a twelve-sided yurt built using wood-framed panelized construction, which includes roof panels in addition to radial rafters.

All of the structural panels for this yurt are built and assembled off-site. Everything can be constructed inside a shop or barn in almost any kind of weather.

When all the components are ready, they can be hauled to the site and set up in a few days. Working off-site also allows the use of power tools that might otherwise not be available for a yurt being built outside of the grid.

The Foundation

Floor Plan

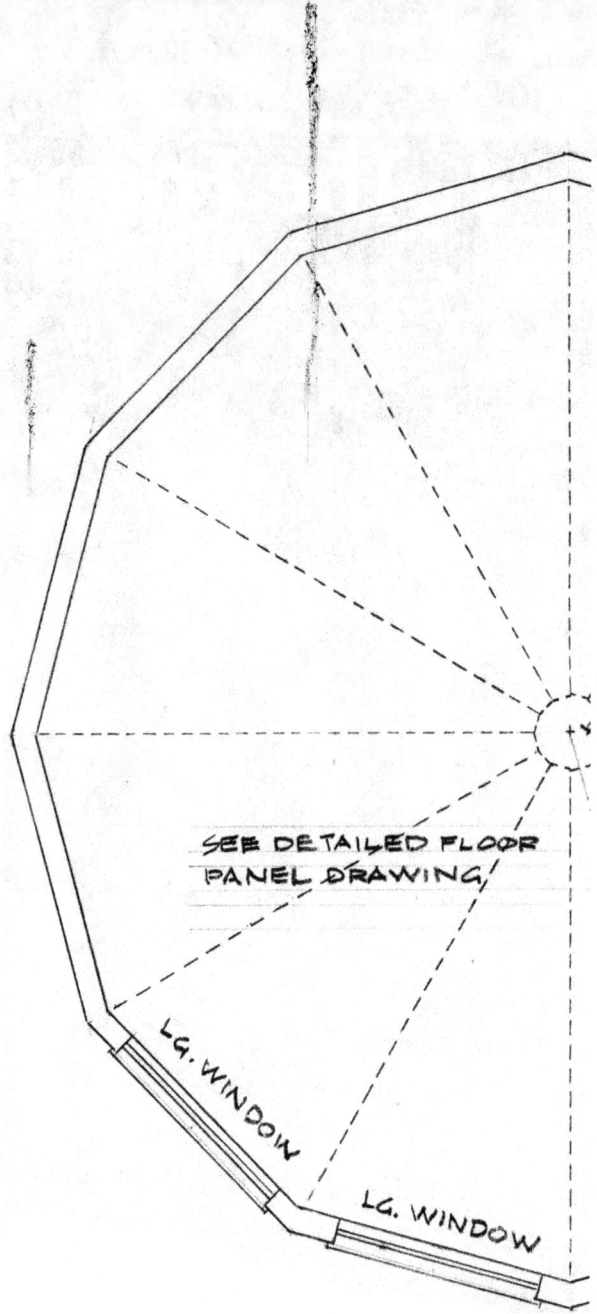

SEE DETAILED FLOOR
PANEL DRAWING.

LG. WINDOW

LG. WINDOW

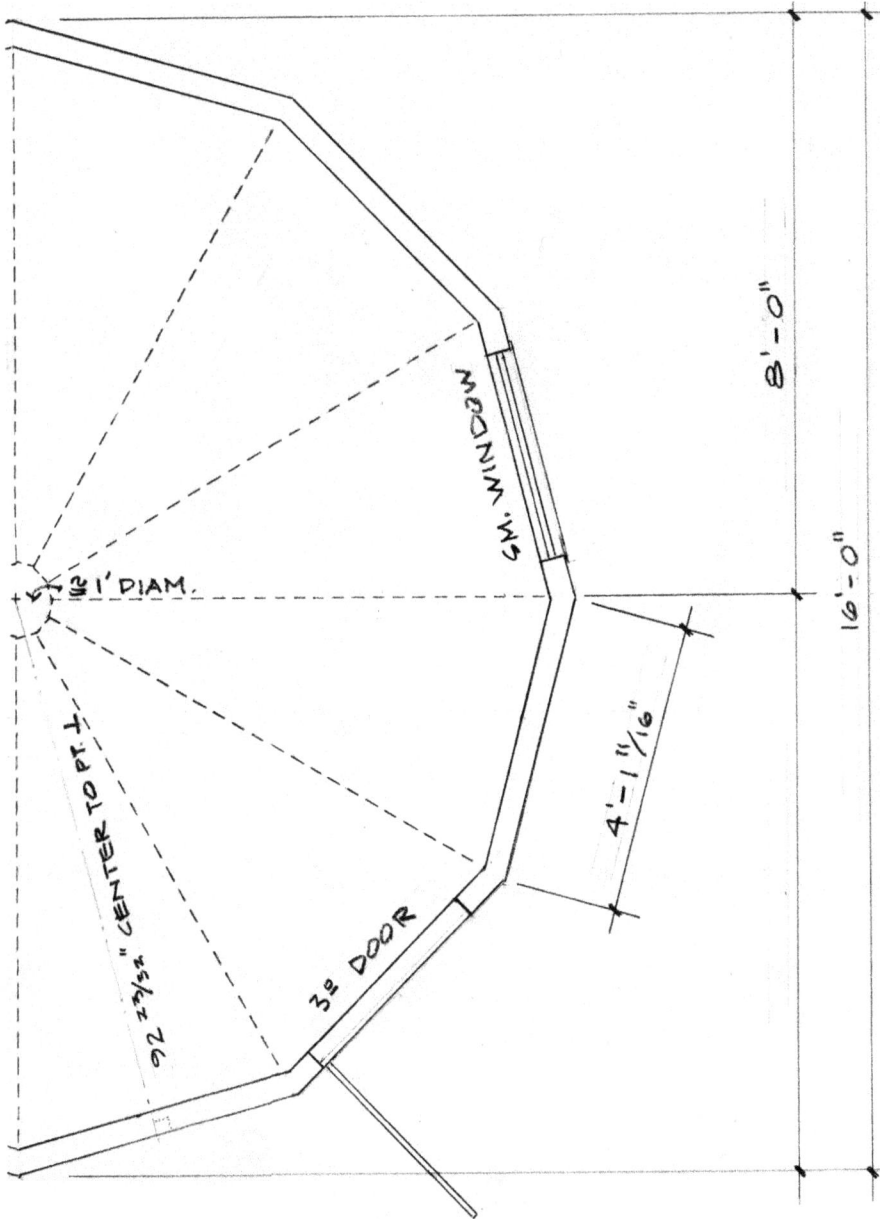

SM. WINDOW

± 1' DIAM.

92 23/32" CENTER TO PT. L.

3" DOOR

8' - 0"

16' - 0"

4' - 1 11/16"

FLOOR PLAN

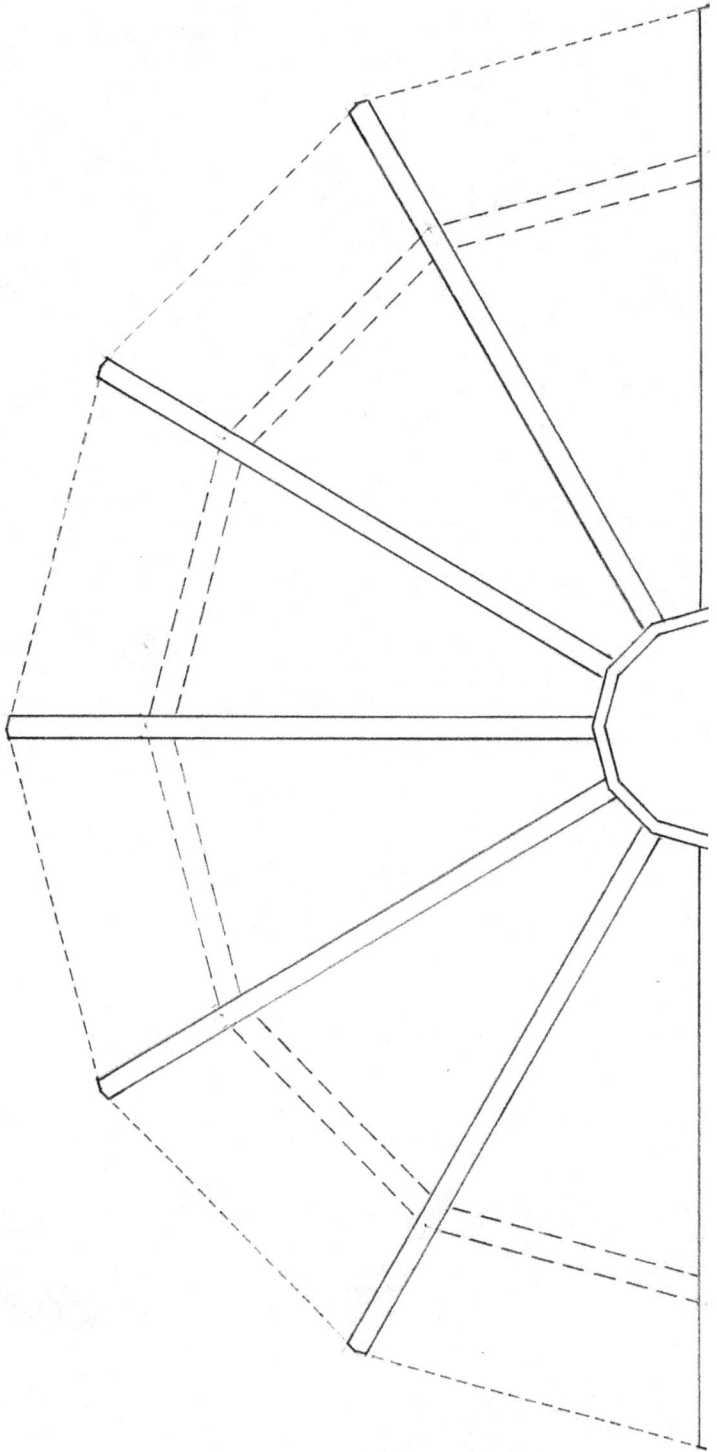

Roof Plan

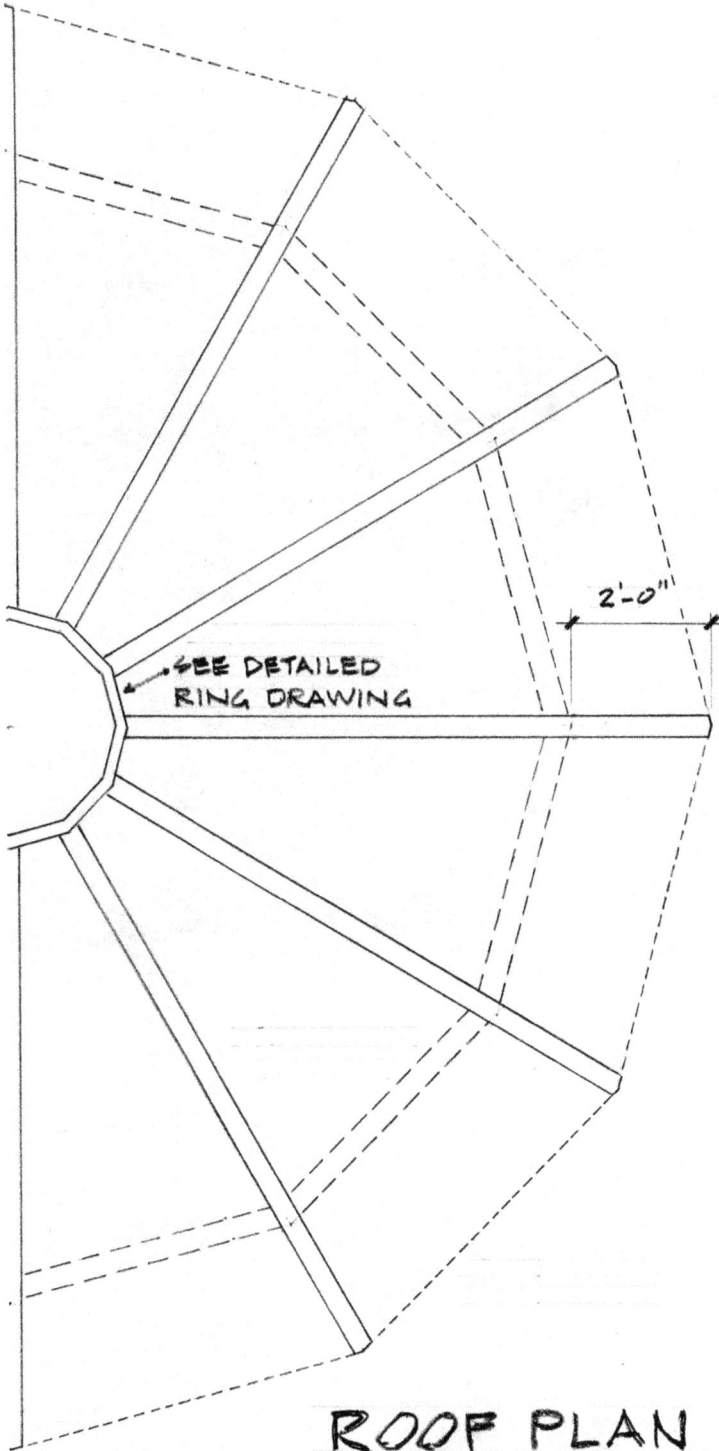

2'-0"

SEE DETAILED
RING DRAWING

ROOF PLAN

Picking a Yurt Site

Yurts can be installed just about anywhere. You just need a way to get everything to where you need it. It makes sense to plan and prepare the site in advance so you can assess any potential issues that might cause you to adjust the yurt size or position. Also as with any building design, consider where doors, windows, deck, etc. will go. Lay out everything and make sure it works before you get started.

The site for our yurt was one of our favorite hang-outs on our property.

Will you electrify the yurt or hook it up to an alternate energy source? Will you plumb it and allow for septic drainage? Unless this is just a camping cabin with no amenities, it's good to consider all of this as you stage the yurt on the building site.

The featured yurt is nestled among ancient western red cedar trees next to a pond on our property. I wanted it to have privacy and nice views of the terrain. I also planned to put a deck in front of the entry door. I worked out all of those details based on the site. Once the site was clear and I had my design figured out, it was time to start building. What I worked on depended on the weather. If it was decent outside, I worked on the foundation. If it was raining, I worked on cutting all the materials and building the panels.

Building the Foundation

You can build any of a number of foundations you want for a yurt. The foundation can depend on the building site, how much excavating you want to do, accessibility, and cost.

The options are as varied as building any house structure, from a slab on grade (level ground), stemwall on footings (possible sloping ground), to posts anchored to concrete piers or all-weather wood (treated) placed on perimeter footings (any terrain).

Pouring a stem wall or a slab foundation will require a lot of concrete but it can be done by hand if you have a team. I won't explain how all of that is done, but it is the system used in several of the larger yurts that I worked on in Oregon and Washington. For this particular yurt, a contractor laid out and poured the foundation.

We will cover only the simplest of foundation applications, which is 12 pier pads with a beam arrangement secured on the tops - a pier and beam foundation system.

If you're thinking of a smaller yurt that is fairly easy to take down and move, it's probably best to do something simple. For my yurt, I used a post to pier and beam system. It was simple, cheap, and worked for the slightly inclined terrain.

Tab is turned to inside so bolting is easier. 15° angle mark is radius line-up.

For the pier and beam system, you can pour your own piers or purchase deck blocks. The pier will be the contact point for the beams. The piers could be further enhanced by combining/tying with a larger concrete pad beneath.

Follow the layout on the following pages.

We had recently dismantled a large deck in front of my shop and had more than enough already fabricated concrete post-piers I could use for the yurt foundation. We also rescued a lot of pressure-treated lumber.

Installing pre-made post-piers isn't something I recommend unless like me, you have some laying around or can get them free. Mine were all different heights plus I had a slight hillside to contend with. The holes would be big because they would have to accommodate the large base. I knew I'd have a good, solid foundation using these, but there were a lot of roots to contend with plus leveling them was no easy chore.

Let's assume you're building this 16' yurt with a pier and beam system as they are usually done – using concrete piers and wood posts or just the piers. The first thing you do for the yurt foundation once you have a cleared spot is lay out the dodecagon, which is the fancy word for a 12-sided shape.

Once you've picked your location and cleared the site, lay out the yurt. Refer to the drawings on pages 20-23.

Armed with 13 stakes or a can of spray paint, start with the center. Rebar is a good option - you can drive it in so you have a secure center. The rest can be stakes or paint. A stake might be more accurate and can be moved easily if you change your mind or make a miscalculation.

As you can see, I opted for spray paint due to the nature of my foundation posts. I was going to be digging a big hole, so a stake wouldn't be much help. I adjusted them once they were in the ground and level. The next step is to cut two measuring sticks, based on the foundation plan.

One stick is the length from the center to a corner: 96″ (8′). The other is the length from one corner to the next corner: 49-5/8″.

Use these sticks to mark your corners, and again to set your pier posts and later, for your beams.

Set your first pier using the measuring stick from the center. I set a center post in first, but a stake is fine. Whatever you do, it is essential to preserve your center exactly where it was when you place the 12 corner piers.

For the next and all the rest of the corners, use both measuring sticks. Measure between corners and from the center. Note that the corners are where the outside edge of the foundation beams will meet. The measurement from the center post is to the center outside face of the post. The measurement for the corner to corner measurement is made from center of post face to center of next post face.

Set and level your pier pads and then recheck everything, using the measuring sticks. You want your foundation to be spot-on so you don't have to deal with inaccuracies later.

The next step is up to you – you can either build your floor system directly on the pier pads using a beam system, or connect pressure treated posts to get the yurt off the ground and/or to deal with a sloped terrain. Since my piers included posts already, once I added some shimming to a few, I was ready to install he foundation beams.

I used pressure-treated beams rescued from the old deck project along with new anchor plates and tie plates. The anchor plates were secured to the posts (which were pre-equipped with bolts) and shimmed to keep them in place.

To note, the foundation beams were all precut along with everything else. As already mentioned, I worked between the shop and the yurt site depending on the weather and other factors. It turned out, I cut all the materials before I began the foundation work. In better weather, I might have just cut the foundation pieces first so I could complete that part of the project.

The center base will need to be up to the level of the beams. The center of the yurt will have a substantial weight load, so you want to allow for that. Be careful not to lose your centerline during this building process.

This photo is a prototype using four concrete pads, four posts and a landing pad as called out in the materials list. I did something different because I was using premade posts.

Use the measuring stick from your foundation layout that is the length from the corner to the center. The beams will replace the other measuring stick that measured from corner to corner. Place the first beam and recheck the measurement to the center using the measuring stick.

If you're happy, put in a screw or two into the anchor plate to stabilize it before moving on.

Bring in the next beam, and follow the same procedure. If your corners are a bit off, you can adjust as you go. Hopefully they are spot-on. Screw in to stabilize.

Once all the beams are placed and looking good, fasten them together with tie plates. Just a couple of screws will work for now. I don't recommend nailing any of this because of the possibility of jarring the structure out of alignment.

When you're done and happy with how it all fits together, finish screwing the plates.

Once the foundation is level and secure, it's time to install the floor panels.

Precutting the Materials

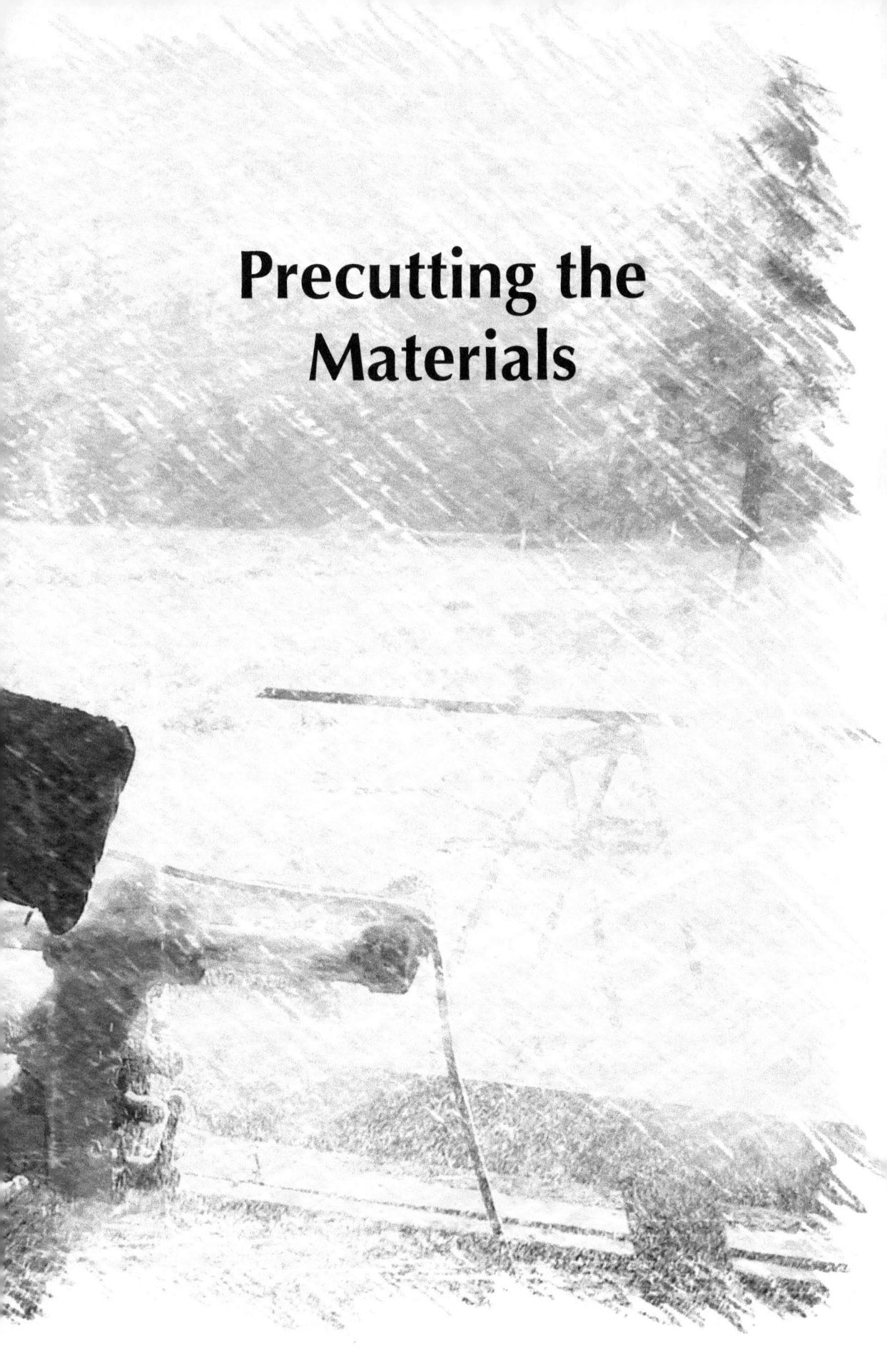

With so many repetitive cuts, it makes sense to precut all the framing before you start building. Organize the pieces so you know what they are all for. It doesn't hurt to label them as well. If you're like me, this was a project I did in spurts between other projects and life in general.

If you're concerned about getting your measurements wrong, mock up one each of the floor (if applicable), wall, and roof panels. Correct any measurements that don't match the drawing and then start cutting. I highly recommend the use of jigs.

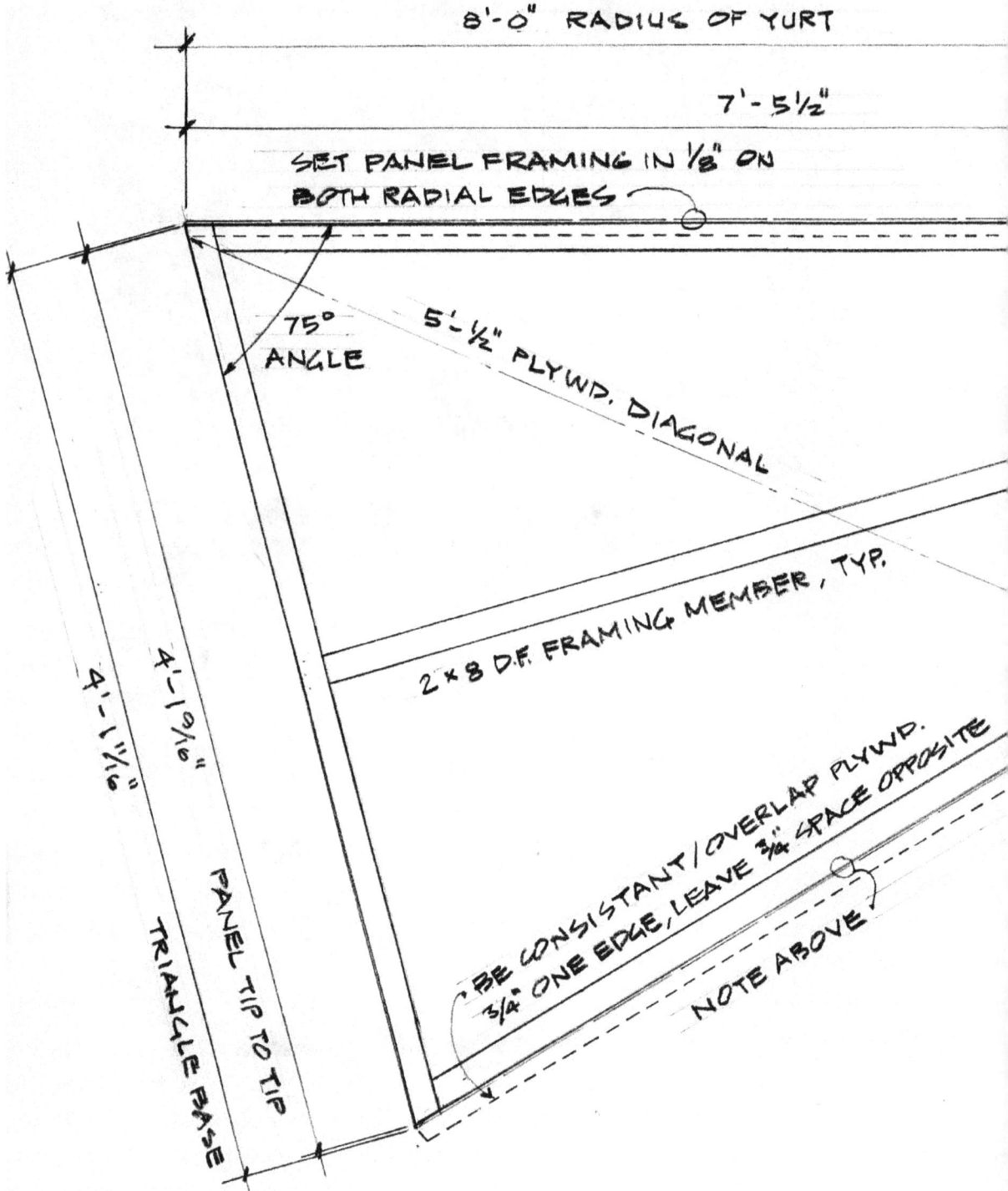

Floor Panel

8'-0" RADIUS OF YURT

7'- 5 ½"

SET PANEL FRAMING IN ⅛" ON
BOTH RADIAL EDGES

75°
ANGLE

5'- ½" PLYWD. DIAGONAL

2 x 8 D.F. FRAMING MEMBER, TYP.

BE CONSISTANT / OVERLAP PLYWD.
¾" ONE EDGE, LEAVE ¾" SPACE OPPOSITE

NOTE ABOVE

4'-1 9/16"

4'-1 1/16"

PANEL TIP TO TIP

TRIANGLE BASE

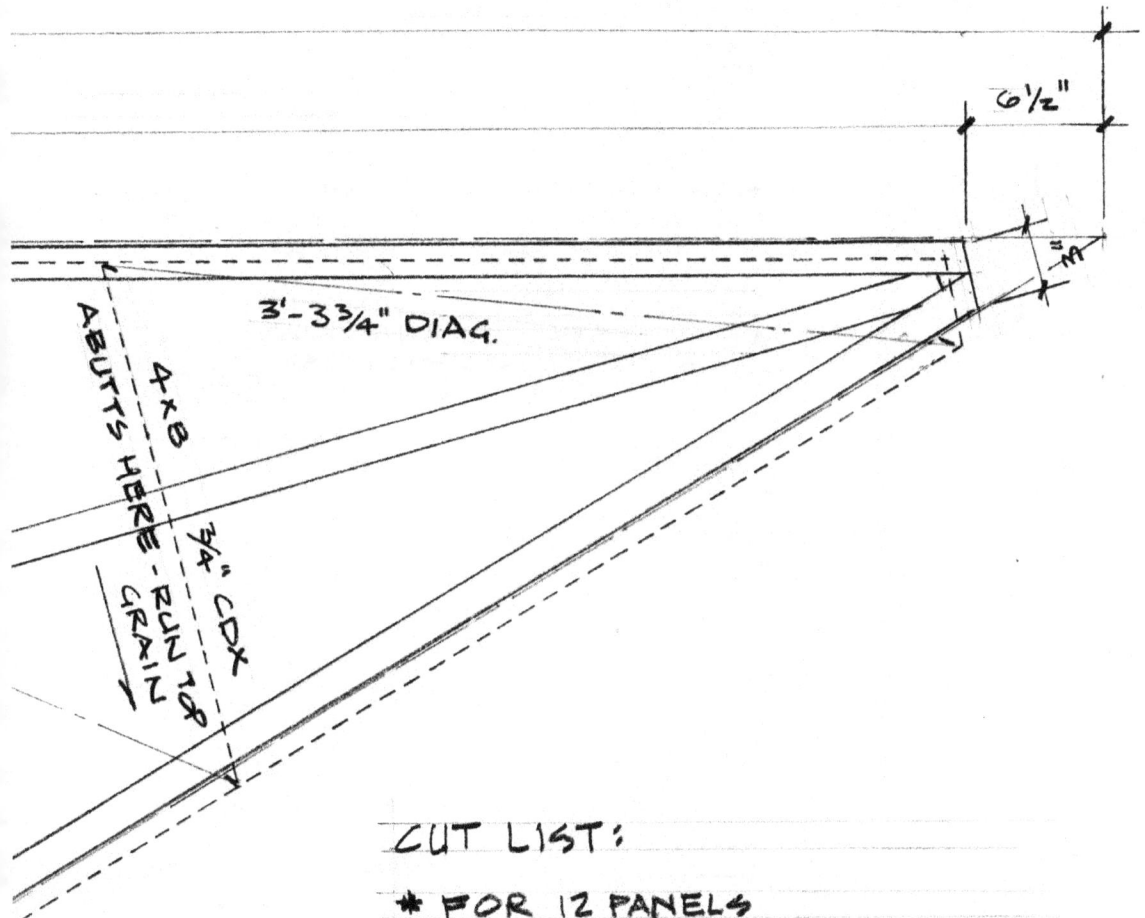

6½"

3'-3¾" DIAG.

4 × 8
ABUTTS HERE - RUN TOP
¾" CDX
GRAIN

CUT LIST:

* FOR 12 PANELS
24 - 2 × 8 AT 7'-5½" SHORT TO
      LONG OF 15° ANGLES, EACH END.
12 - 2 × 8 AT 7'-0"
      (NOTE TAPER AT ONE END.)
12 - 2 × 8 AT 4'-1⁹⁄₁₆" LONG END
      TO LONG END OF 15° ANGLES,
      BOTH ENDS

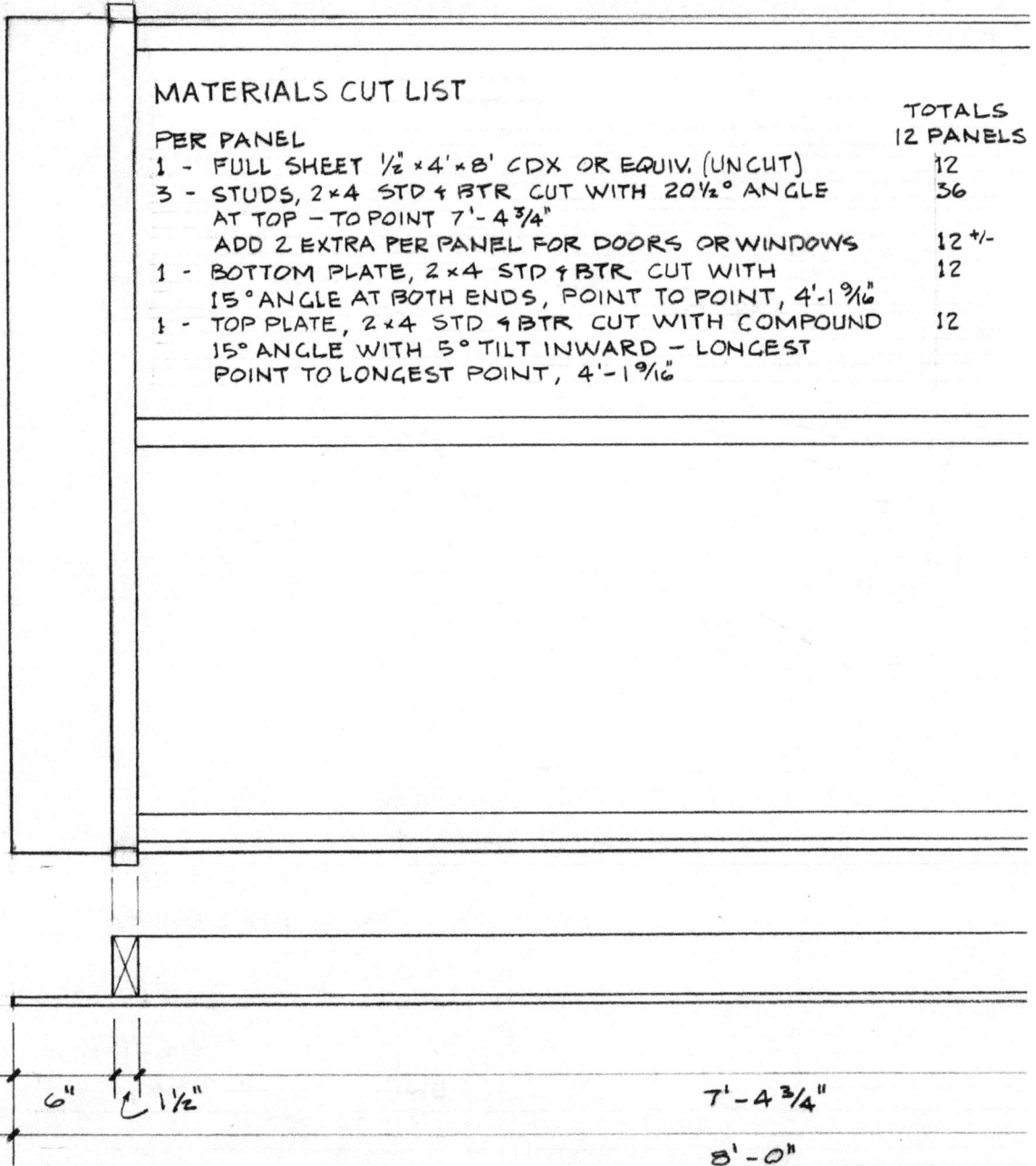

Wall Panel

MATERIALS CUT LIST

		TOTALS
PER PANEL		12 PANELS
1 - FULL SHEET ½" × 4' × 8' CDX OR EQUIV. (UNCUT)		12
3 - STUDS, 2×4 STD & BTR CUT WITH 20½° ANGLE AT TOP — TO POINT 7'- 4¾"		36
ADD 2 EXTRA PER PANEL FOR DOORS OR WINDOWS		12 +/-
1 - BOTTOM PLATE, 2×4 STD & BTR CUT WITH 15° ANGLE AT BOTH ENDS, POINT TO POINT, 4'-1 9/16"		12
1 - TOP PLATE, 2×4 STD & BTR CUT WITH COMPOUND 15° ANGLE WITH 5° TILT INWARD — LONGEST POINT TO LONGEST POINT, 4'-1 9/16"		12

6"   1½"   7'- 4¾"

8'- 0"

WALL PANEL

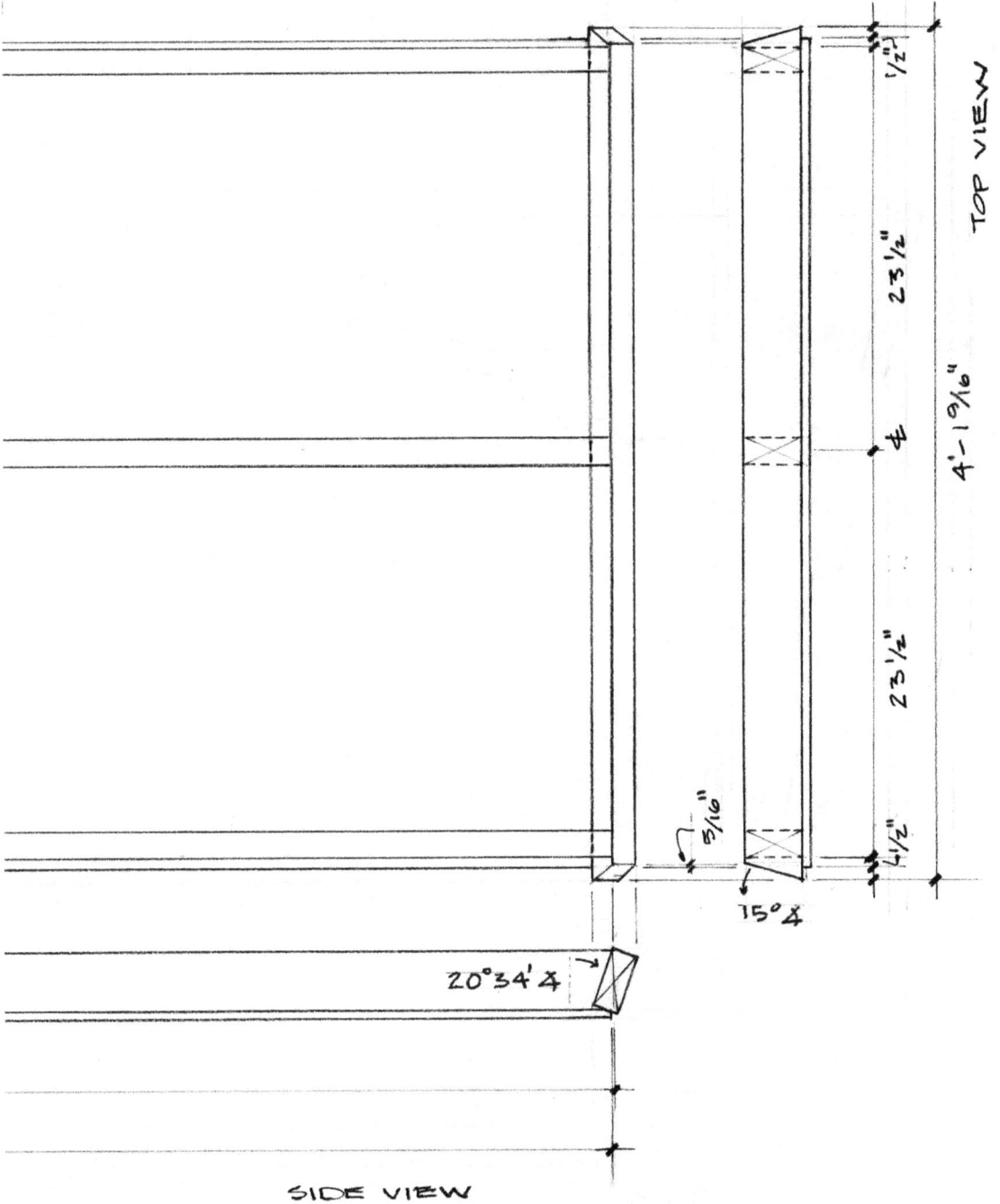

5/16"

20°34' ⌐

15° ⌐

1/2"

23 1/2"

⌐

23 1/2"

4 1/2"

4'-19/16"

TOP VIEW

SIDE VIEW

SCALE

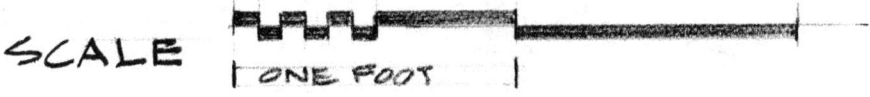

ONE FOOT

Roof Panel

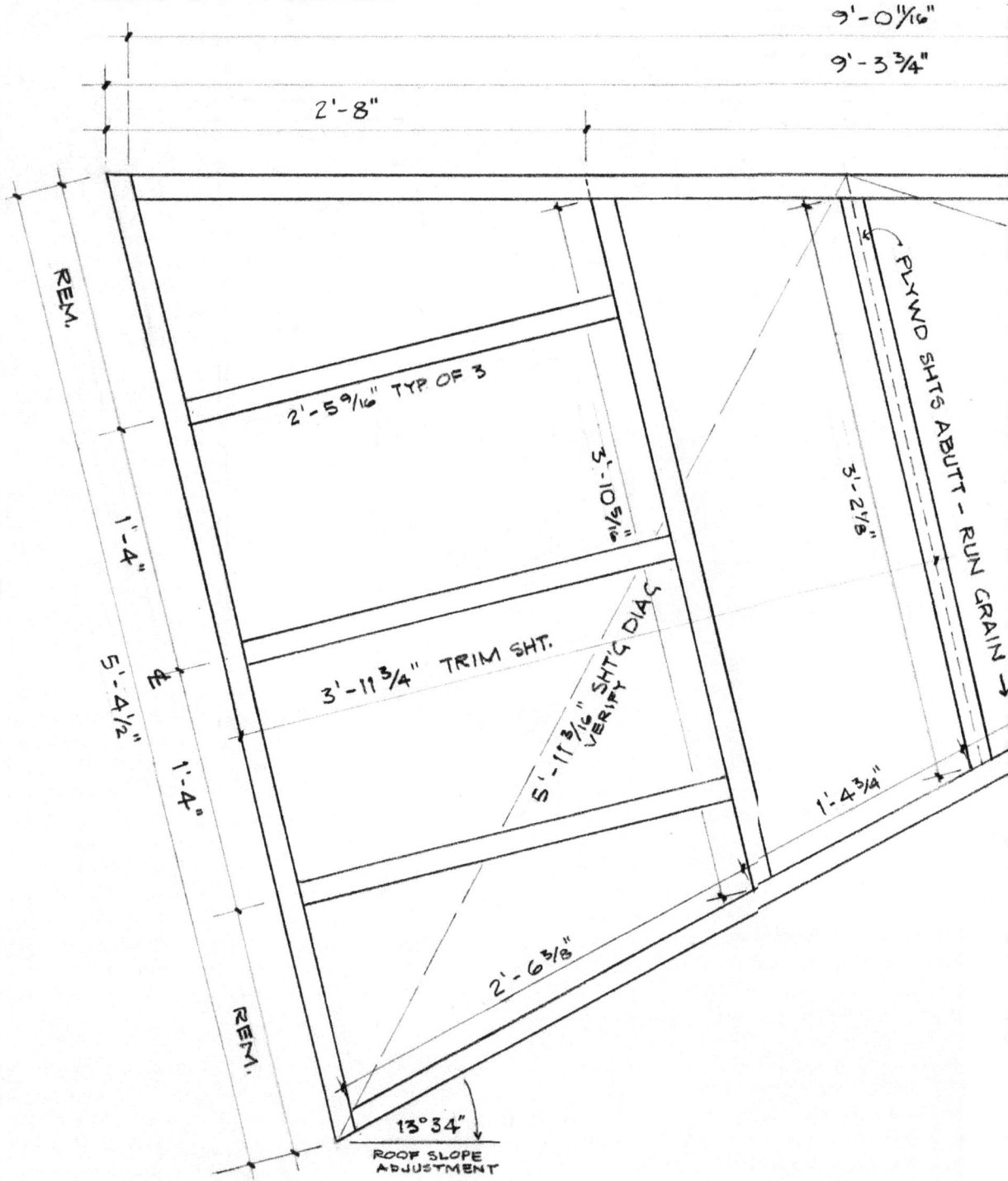

9'-0 11/16"

9'-3 3/4"

2'-8"

REM.

PLYWD SHTS ABUTT - RUN GRAIN →

2'-5 9/16" TYP OF 3

3'-10 5/16"

3'-2 1/8"

1'-4"

5'-4 1/2"

3'-11 3/4" TRIM SHT.

5'-11 3/16" SHT'G DIAG
VERIFY

1'-4"

1'-4 3/4"

REM.

2'-6 3/8"

13° 34"

ROOF SLOPE
ADJUSTMENT

SCALE: 1 FOOT

6' - 7¾"

10⁷⁄₁₆"

FILL WITH REMAINDER

4' - 8³⁄₁₆" SHT'G DIAG VERIFY

1' - 10⅛"

1' - 2⅛"

1' - 4½"

2' - 6⅛"

1' - 4½"

1' - 4½"

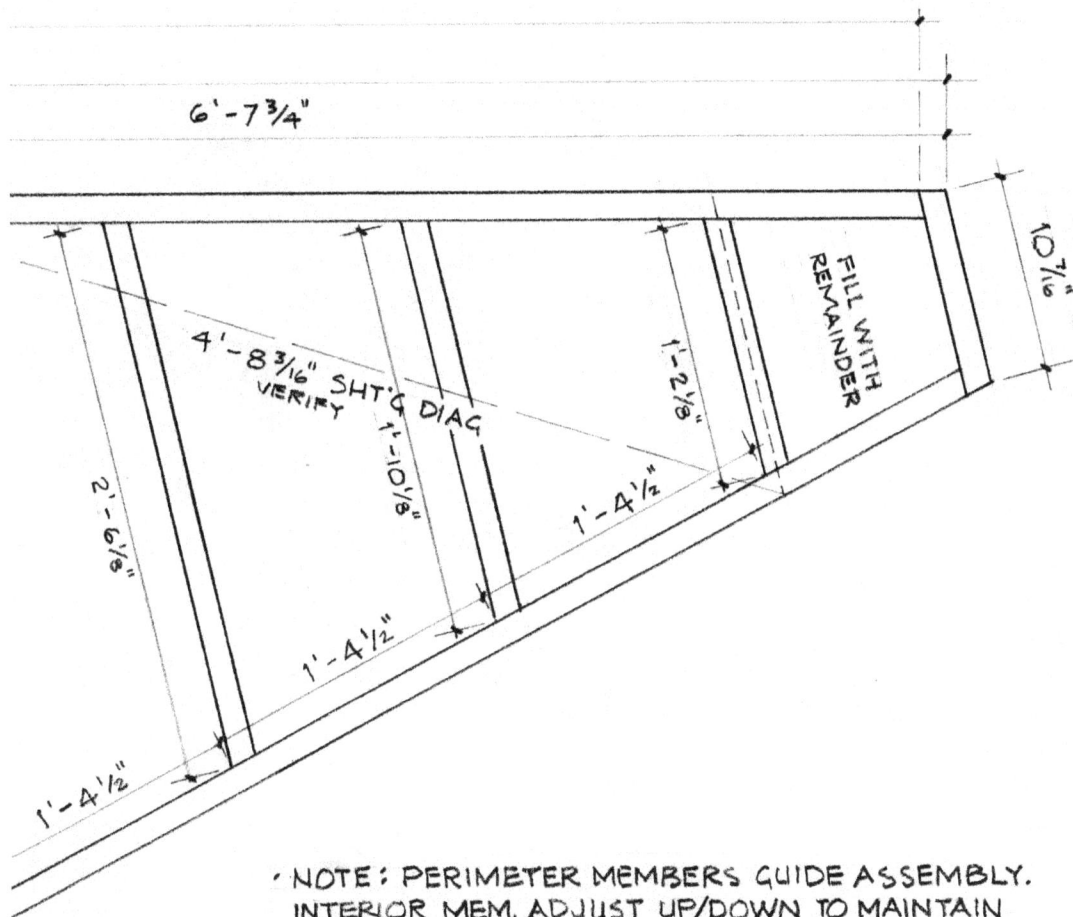

· NOTE: PERIMETER MEMBERS GUIDE ASSEMBLY.
INTERIOR MEM. ADJUST UP/DOWN TO MAINTAIN
STRAIGHT SIDES.

CUT LIST:

· 60 - 2×4 -10' STD & BTR D.F. (OR 2×6 IF EXTRA
INSULATION). NOTE: RING SET UP FOR 2×6
FRAMING — SEE RING DRAWING.
· CUT 12 OF EACH/EVERY MEMBER IN THIS DRAW'G.
· GROUP "CUTS" TO OPTIMIZE LUMBER USE, I.E.
1 - 9'-0⁷⁄₁₆" = 1 -10' // "CUTS" 46⁵⁄₁₆" + 38⅛" + 30⅛" =
114⁹⁄₁₆" = 1 - 10'

ROOF PANEL

Skylight Dome

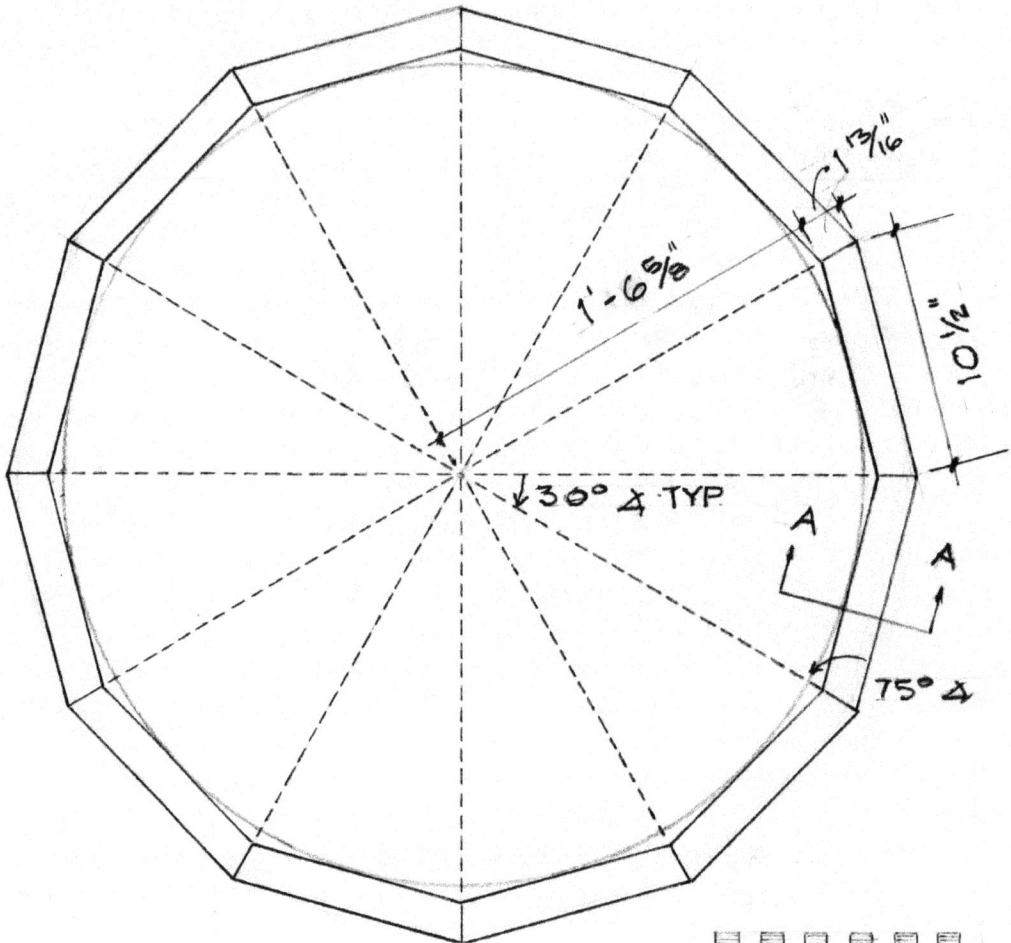

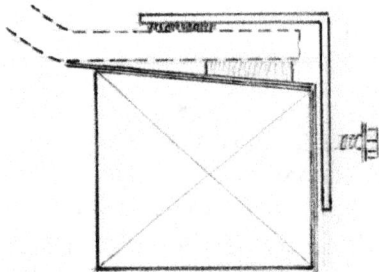

1'-6⅝"

1¹³⁄₁₆"

10½"

30° ⊿ TYP

A   A

75° ⊿

SCALE: 1 FOOT
         INCHES

· 1½" × 1¾" RING SEG-
MENT, W/5° SLOPE.
· 2" × 3" CAP FLASH'G.
· 1½" × 1½" × ¹⁄₁₆" ALU-
MINUM CAP PIECE.

SECTION A-A

CUT LIST:

· 1 2×4 6'/8' DECKWOOD,
RIP 2 LENGTHS 1¾"
WIDE. CUT 12 SEGMENTS
10½" LONG, POINT TO
POINT OF 15° ⊿ ENDS.
TAPER TOP 5° SLOPE.
· 12 FT. 1½" × 1½" × ¹⁄₁₆" ALUMINUM
ANGLE, CUT 12 PCS. AS
ABOVE

1'-8 7/16"

30° ∠ TYP.

CUT 1/8" INSIDE
OF LINE

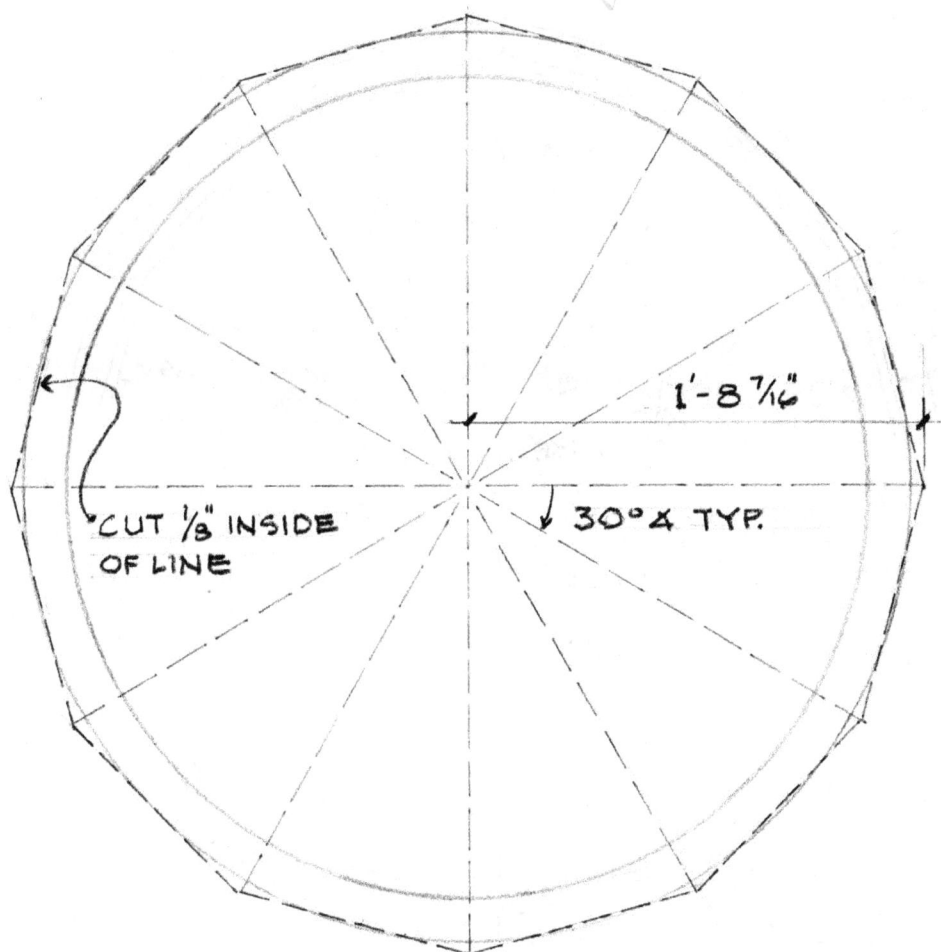

MAKE TEMPLATE LAYOUT AS ABOVE
FROM CARDBOARD OR PLYWOOD.
PLACE 3' DIA. SKYLIGHT OVER
AND CUT OFF FLANGE 1/8" IN-
SIDE OF 12 BOUNDARY LINES.

Rafter Ring

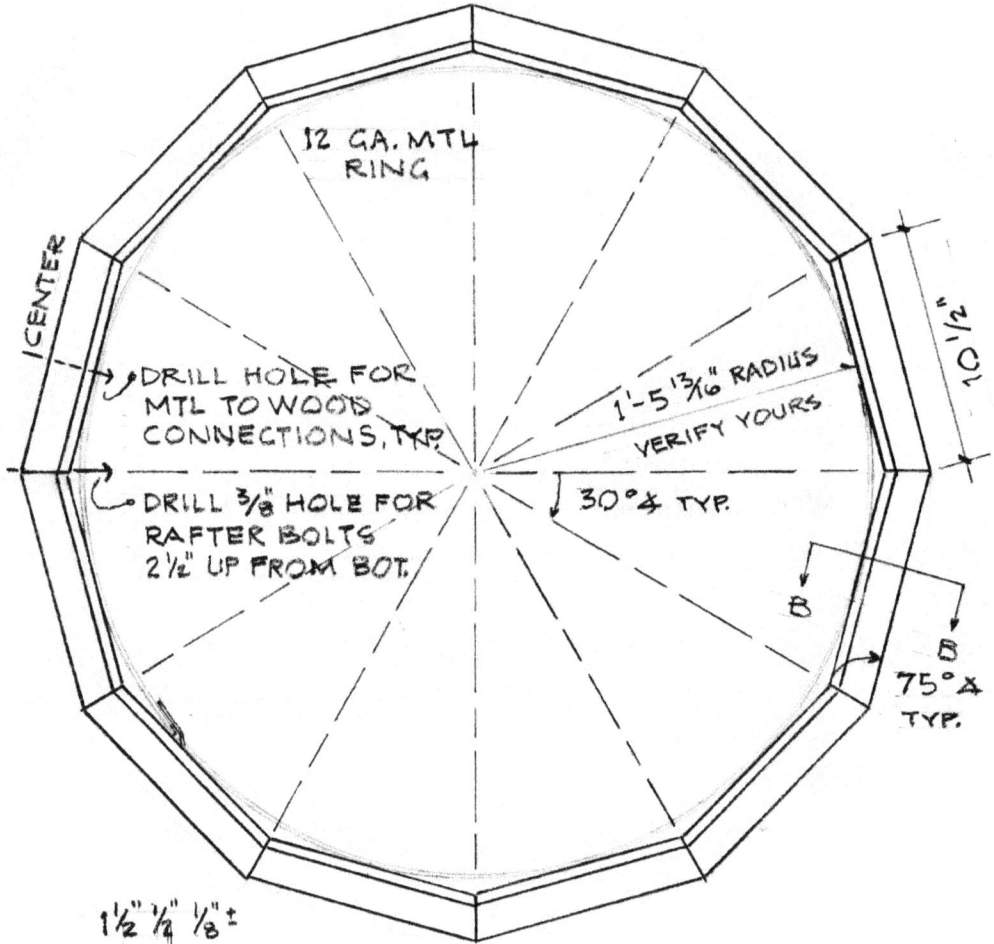

12 GA. MTL RING

CENTER

DRILL HOLE FOR MTL TO WOOD CONNECTIONS, TYP.

DRILL 3/8" HOLE FOR RAFTER BOLTS 2 1/2" UP FROM BOT.

1'-5 13/16" RADIUS VERIFY YOURS

30°& TYP.

10 1/2"

B

B 75° & TYP.

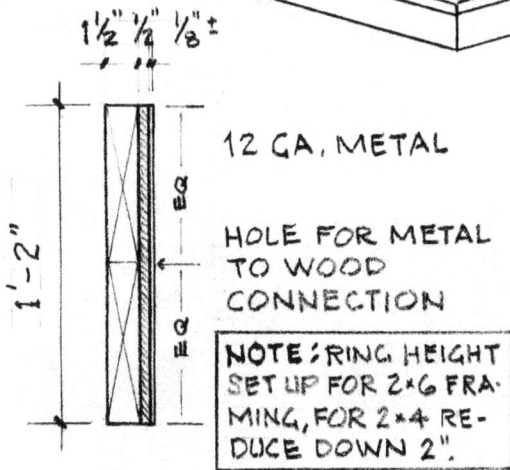

1 1/2" 1/2" 1/8"±

12 GA. METAL

HOLE FOR METAL TO WOOD CONNECTION

EQ

EQ

1'-2"

NOTE: RING HEIGHT SET UP FOR 2×6 FRAMING, FOR 2×4 REDUCE DOWN 2".

CUT LIST:
- 2 - 2×8-12' KD (OPTION'L, TO PREVENT WARPAGE) D.F. RIP EACH TO TOTAL 14"
- 1 SHT 1/2" CDX PLYWD. RIP 14" STRIPS. FACE GLUE TO ABOVE 2×8's
- CUT COMBINED WITH OUTER DIMEN. AT 10 1/2" POINT TO POINT OF 15° &

SECTION B-B

SCALE: 1 FT.

RING

Rafter

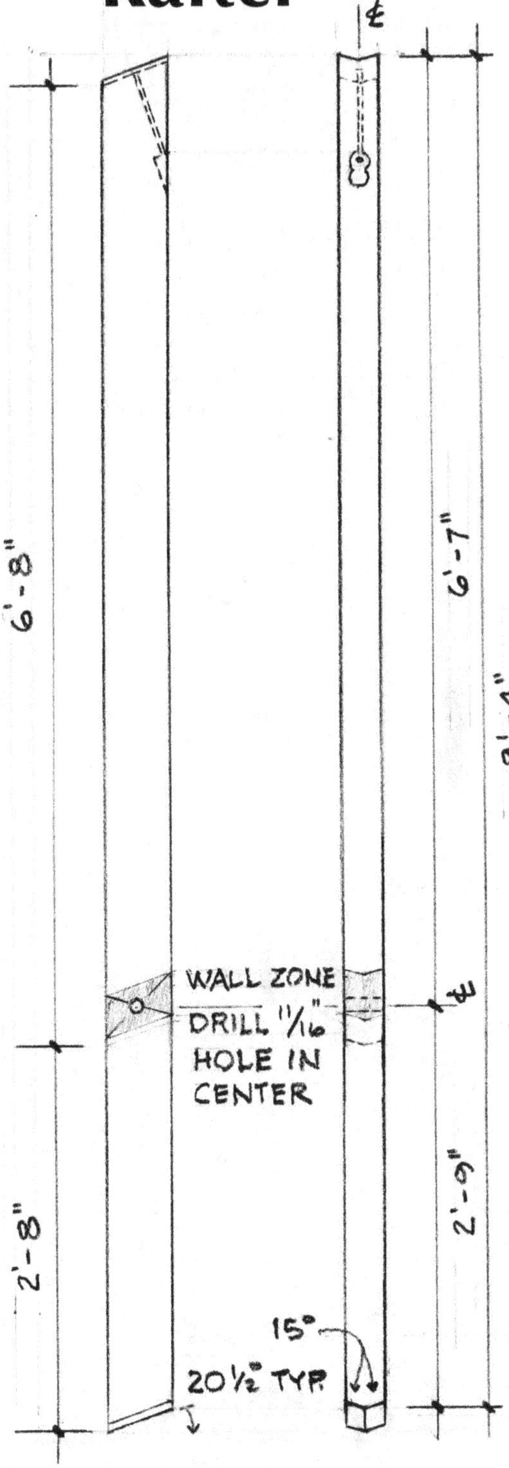

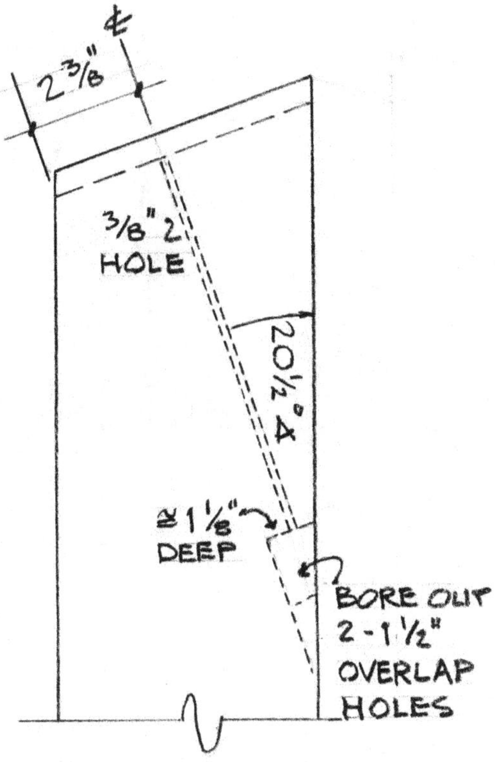

6'-8"

7°

6'-7"

9'-4"

2'-3⁄8"

3⁄8" 2
HOLE

20½° 4

≅1⅛"
DEEP

BORE OUT
2 - 1½"
OVERLAP
HOLES

RING END DETAIL

WALL ZONE
DRILL "¹¹⁄₁₆"
HOLE IN
CENTER

2'-8"

2'-9"

15°

20½° TYP.

CUT LIST:
- 12 - 4 × 6 -10' D.F. STD &
  BTR. CUT ENDS WITH
  COMPOUND ANGLES

RAFTERS

Tower

FRAME "A" LADDER SIDES AS SHOWN (BUILD 2), STAND ON
ON EDGE, TIES & BRACING OUTWARD, NAIL/SCREW ON "B"
CROSSTIES, BRACE INTERNALLY, ROLL TO 2ND "B" SIDE, FASTEN.

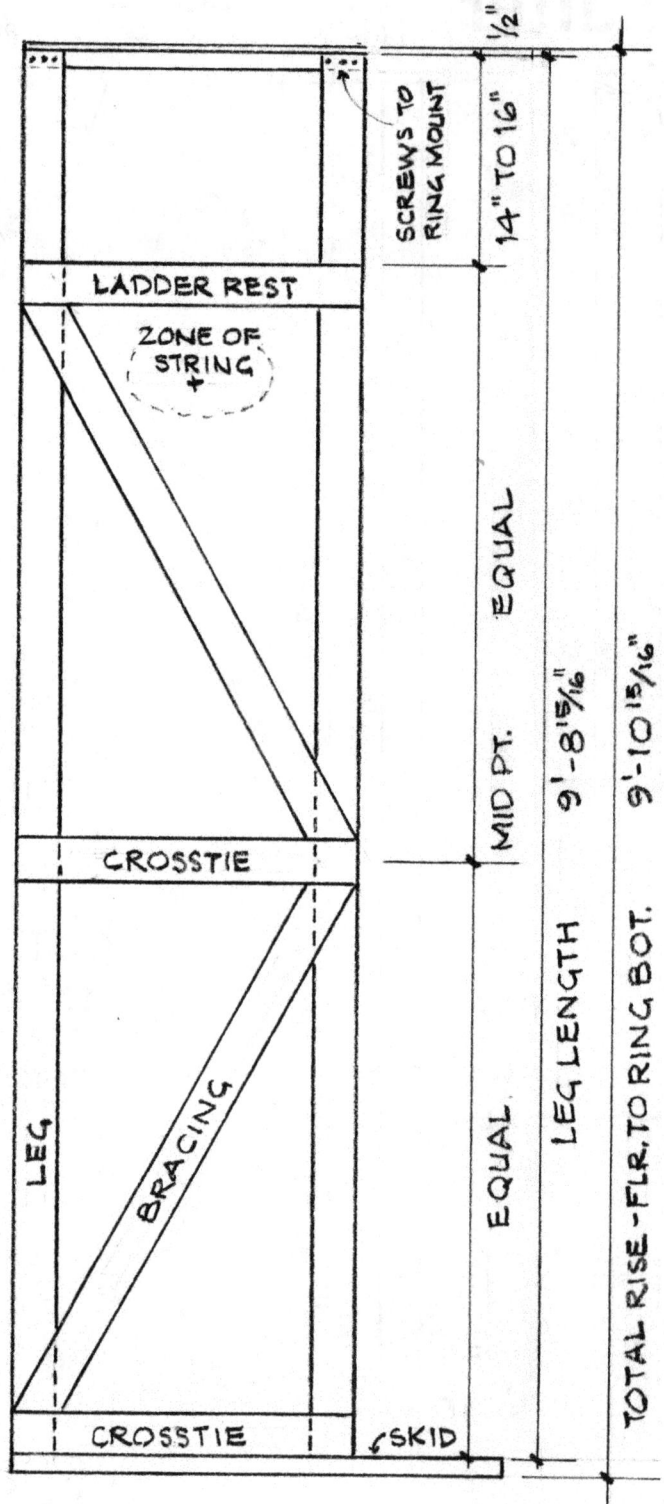

LADDER REST

ZONE OF
STRING
+

CROSSTIE

LEG

BRACING

CROSSTIE   SKID

SCREWS TO RING MOUNT

½"

14" TO 16"

EQUAL

MID PT.   9'-8¹⁵/₁₆"

EQUAL   LEG LENGTH

9'-10¹⁵/₁₆"

TOTAL RISE - FLR. TO RING BOT.

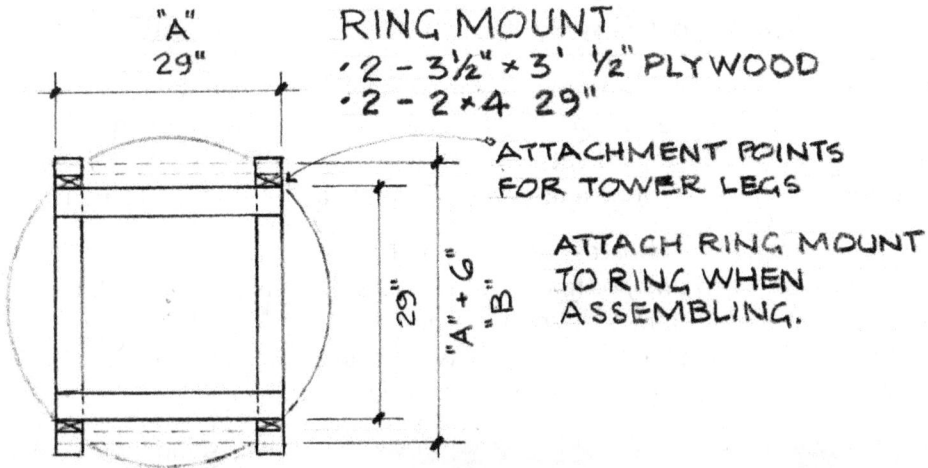

RING MOUNT
- 2 - 3½" × 3' ½" PLYWOOD
- 2 - 2×4 29"

"A" 29"

29"

"A" + 6" "B"

ATTACHMENT POINTS FOR TOWER LEGS

ATTACH RING MOUNT TO RING WHEN ASSEMBLING.

TOWER CUT LIST
- FROM 10 - 10' D.F.
- 4 LEGS
- 6 "A" CROSSTIES
- 6 "B" CROSSTIES
- 4 BRACINGS

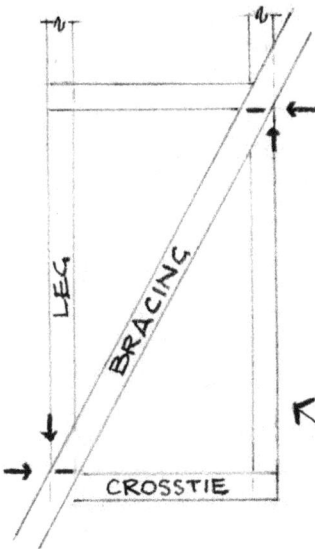

FRAME "A" SIDE (LADDER) W/CROSS-TIES, CHECK DIAGONALS, STAB-ILIZE, THEN NAIL IN BRACING.

NOTE: TIPS OF SKIDS ACT AS BRAKES WHEN RAISING TOWER. POINT UP. RAISE TOWER WITH BRACING IN LINE WITH LIFT DIRECTION.

LEG

BRACING

CROSSTIE

ROLL TO DO 2ND "B" SIDE

LIFT

BRACING A LINES TIPS UP

SCREWS TO RING MOUNT AFTER COMPLETE ALL FRAMING, EX-CEPT SKIDS.

2X SKIDS 3½' LONG PLACE ON LAST, AFTER ATTACH'G TO RING.

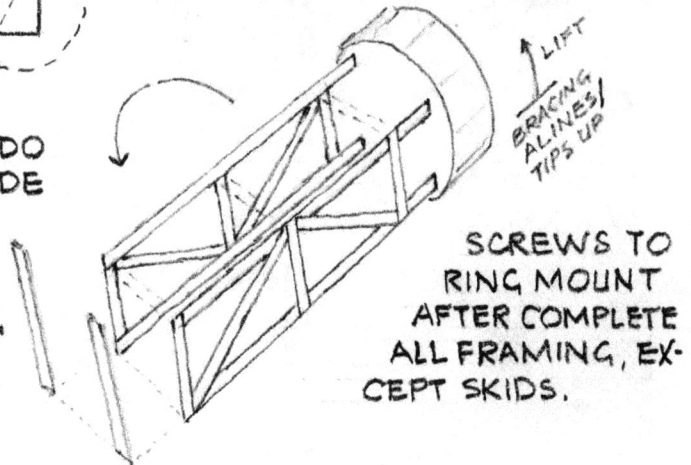

Making a Quick and Simple "Stop" for Multiple Cuts

With all of those repetitive cuts, many of them angled, jigs can save a lot of time and maintain accuracy. I can then run the boards through fairly quickly. When making multiple angled cuts on one board: start with one end, cut angle, bump angle to the stop, cut next angle, bump angle to the stop, and so on.

When I'm cutting a lot of boards the same length and angle, it doesn't make sense to measure each time, or mark multiple cuts along a single board. Employing a block stop system is not only efficient, it also allows the boss to set up a cut and turn someone loose on the task who knows how to safely run the saw and won't have to worry about careful measuring.

Use scrap wood – 2 pieces of 2x material + a piece of 3/4" material (plus whatever needed) to create a support that is at the same level as the cutoff saw's table base. In this photo a layer of cardboard was used under the 3/4" material to obtain the right level.

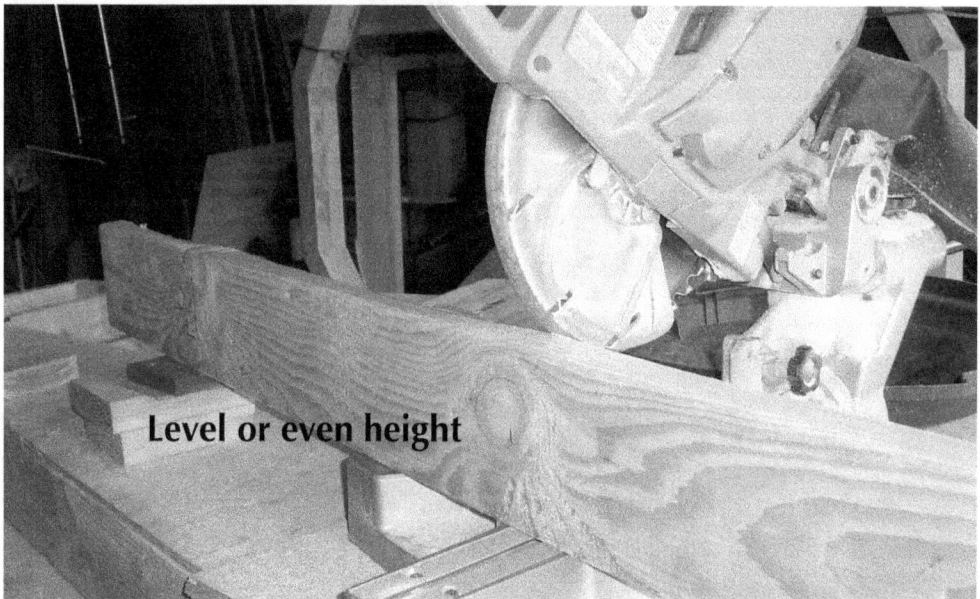

Level or even height

Check that the table of the saw is at the same level as the "stop" support base. With the cut-off saw secured to the work table, square up one end of a board and mark it for your proper length to be cut multiple times, creating your **set-up board.**

Lay the set-up board so the length mark is directly under the blade. Center the support base under the other end. Fasten both 2x scraps down securely to the work table. Leave the 3/4" scrap loose for now.

Nick the set-up board with the blade at the length mark as a test for accuracy. No need to cut it to length, you might have a use for it elsewhere.

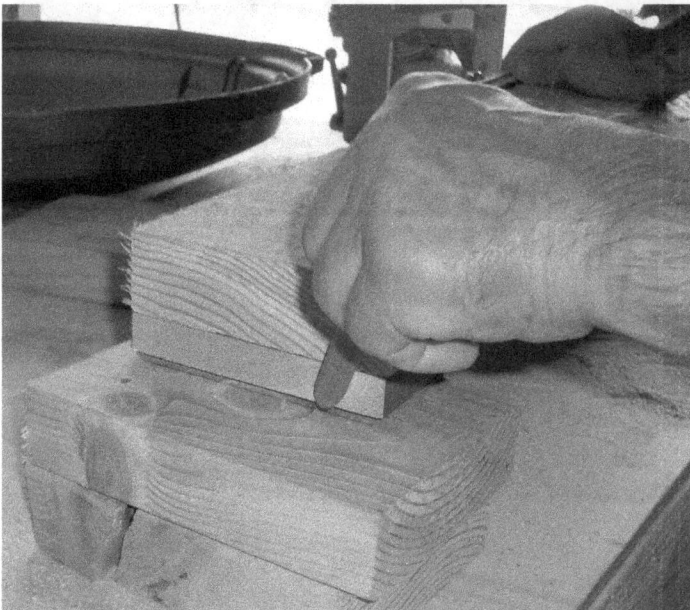

Keeping the set-up board held securely, flush edges with the 3/4" scrap. Pencil mark the 2x support base.

Fasten the 3/4″ scrap to the 2x support base at your pencil mark: the end of this board is your stop length.

Use a straight cut scrap to flush the 3/4″ stop board edge with the board to be cut. Start cutting! If you are cutting angles, just make sure the tip of the angle hits the stop block. Otherwise you risk undermining.

I also used a jig system for the wall panel assembly, which I'll explain when we get to the chapter on wall panels.

Floor Panels

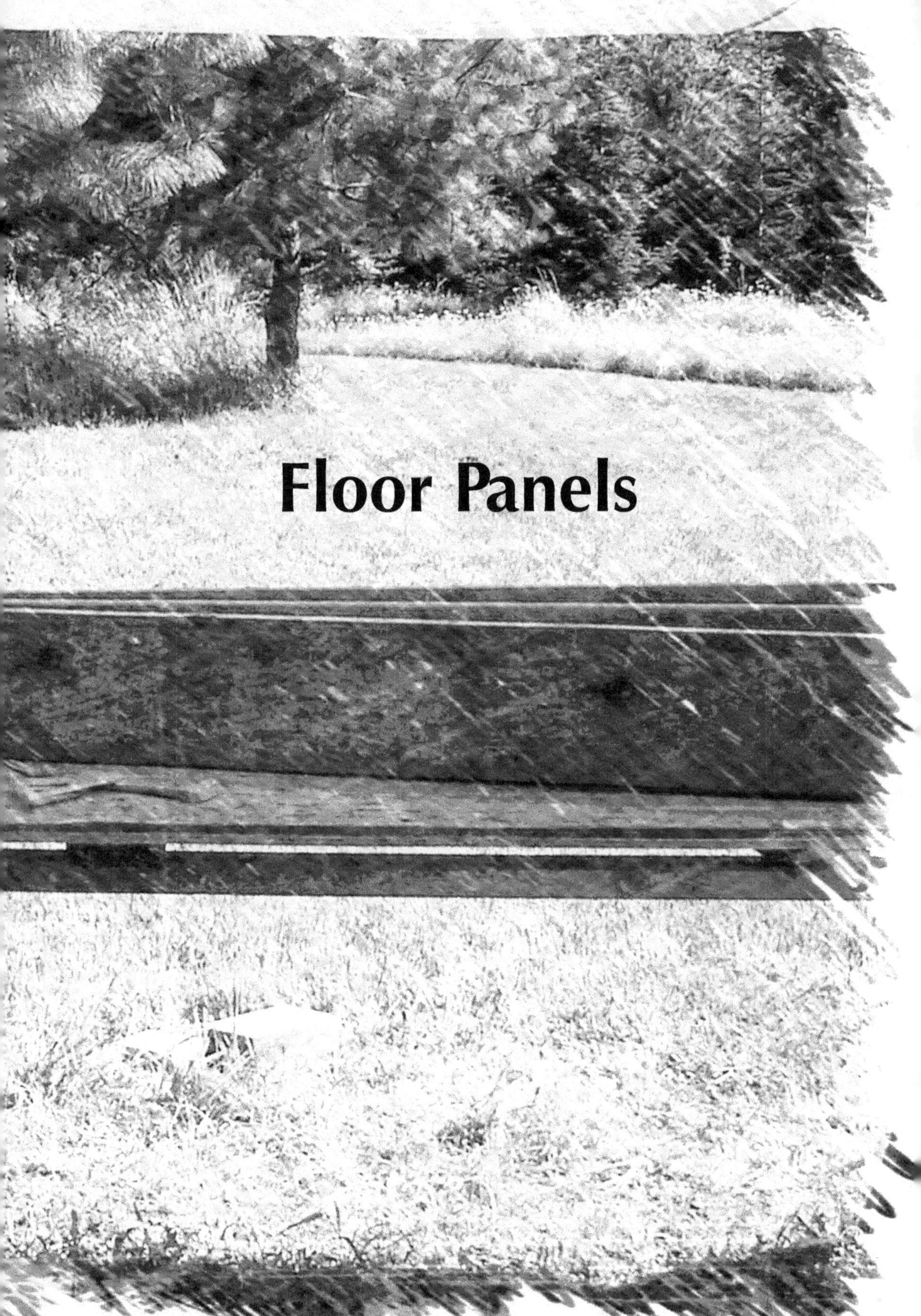

I elected to build 12 floor panels rather than install a joist and plywood floor system in order to demonstrate how a complete yurt can be built off-site. The first step is to get your precut pieces organized and start your assembly. Note that the middle pieces will need some cheek cuts during assembly.

Referring to the drawing on page 38, lay out the three outside pieces in a triangle. Check for crowned boards and put the crown side up. Use a straight edge to check the sides. If one or both are bowed, aim the bow to the inside. You can deal with it later before attaching the plywood. It's easy to wedge-push it out if needed.

Nail the two side pieces together at the bottom, and clamp them at the top. Keep all the top edges flush to meet up neatly with the plywood.

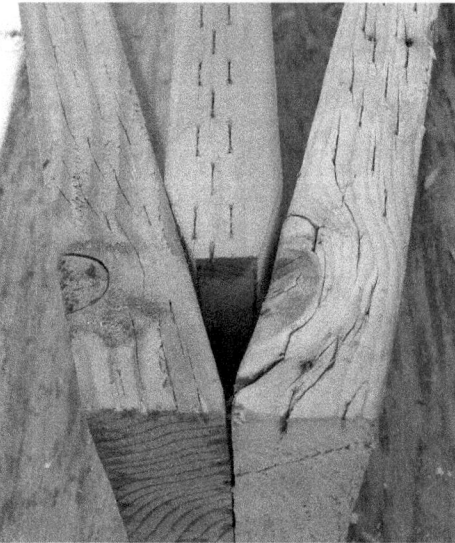

The middle piece requires two cheek cuts so that it fits snugly, giving you something solid to nail to.

Check out the video listed at the end of the book if you want to see that process.

To get the most out of your sheet of plywood, plan your layout to be across the sheet, so that the top grain will run parallel to your panel buttom.

The photo shows my planning the numbers of the two pieces that make up the subfloor.

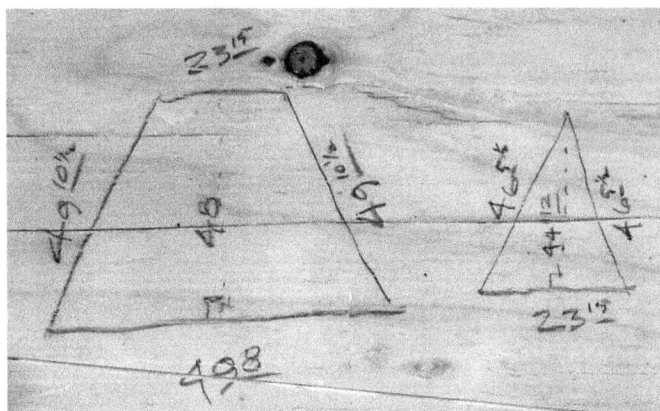

Refer back to the floor panel drawing for the diagonals that are used to check for accuracy. Verify this as yours may be slightly different. The two diagonal measurements should be equal.

I set my saw to the thickness of the plywood so I can cut on a flat surface, in this case, plywood layers on saw horses.

Before nailing the plywood, recheck the sides for bows. If you have any, now is the time to deal with them before you nail on the plywood. See the sidebar on pg. 62 for how I deal with bows.

During yurt assembly, the floor panels tie together with a 3/4″ tab you create during this process of making them.

You can do this by screwing down a 3/4″ stick along the length of one side. Be sure to do all the panels on the same side. This 3/4″ piece is removed after the floor sheathing is nailed on.

Run a bead of construction adhesive before putting down the plywood. This makes for a sturdy floor system.

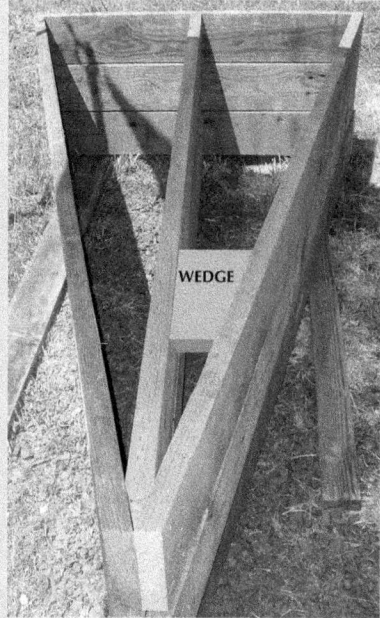

Dealing with bows

Lumber is never perfectly straight. Because we put our bows toward the inside, all we have to do now is use a tapered block of wood as a wedge to push out the side. Turn the panel over and remove the wedge after everything is nailed off.

Find your framing centerlines and mark or snap a line. Mark your layout measuring stick with bold dots for your nail pattern. Use this guide to do a neat, fast job. I placed the floor nails (8d ringshank) 6″ apart.

Carry on with the same procedure for the top plywood piece. Notice the overlap plywood edge above. Keep this to the same side of each panel. Remember to remove the 3/4" spacer piece (top photo) after plywood has been nailed on. The side also determines which way the panels will lay in. This is set up to rotate right as you go around during assembly. The panel to the right overlapping the already placed panel to the left.

Install insulation. I used R21 for the floor panels.

Fasten on a protective barrier of some kind to help keep the critters out. I used 1/4"x1/4" galvanized hardware cloth which I stapled to the inside with polyester strapping tape overlay.

If necessary, shim the boards so they are flush at the bearing points (tip). That way they seat nicely on the center post. My floor pieces came from various sources and some varied slightly in width. A few bits of asphalt roofing did the trick. I use a plastic scrap between the roofing and the staple to prevent break-through.

Once the floor panels were done, I hauled them to the yurt site, all ready to be installed.

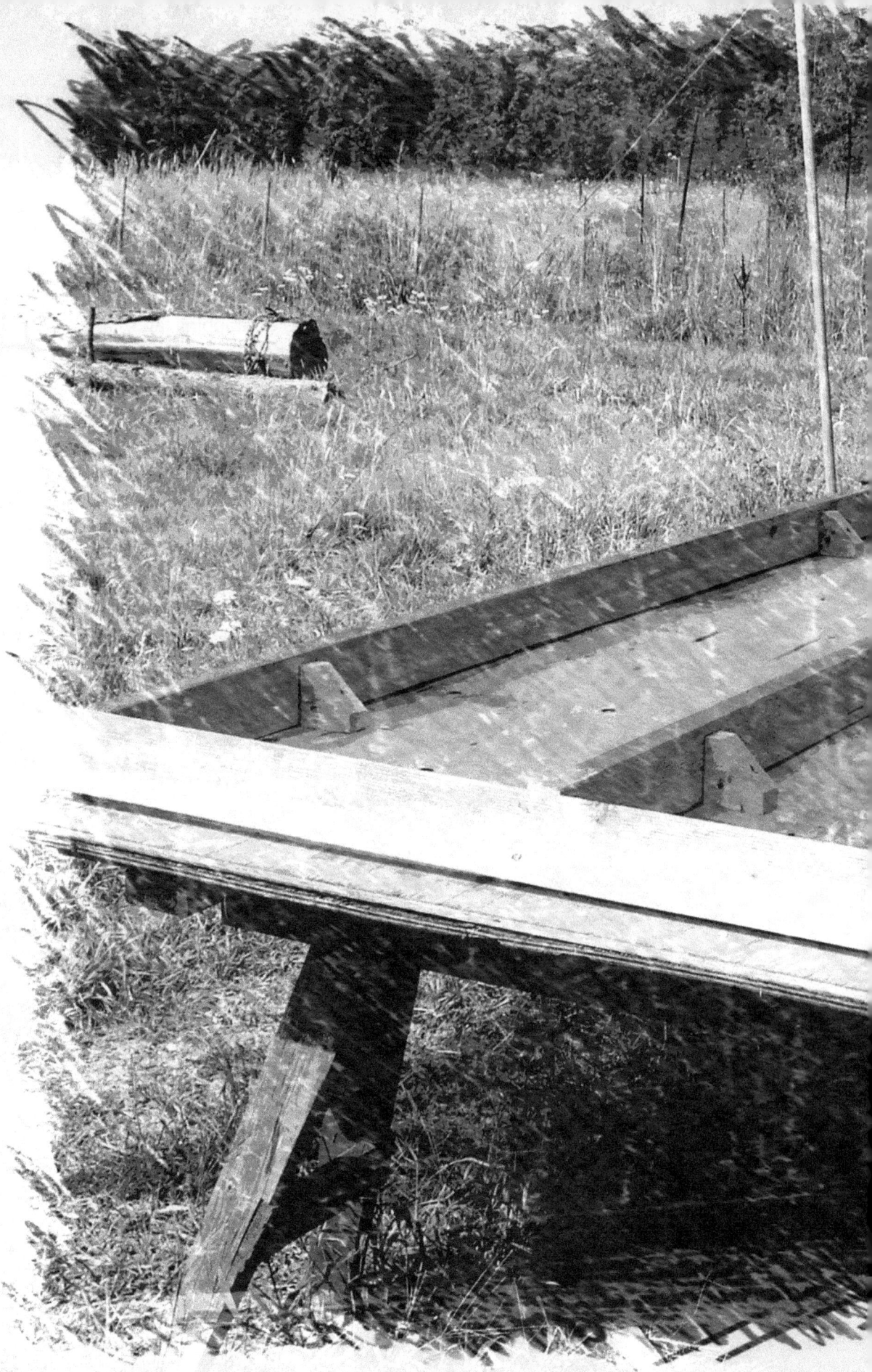

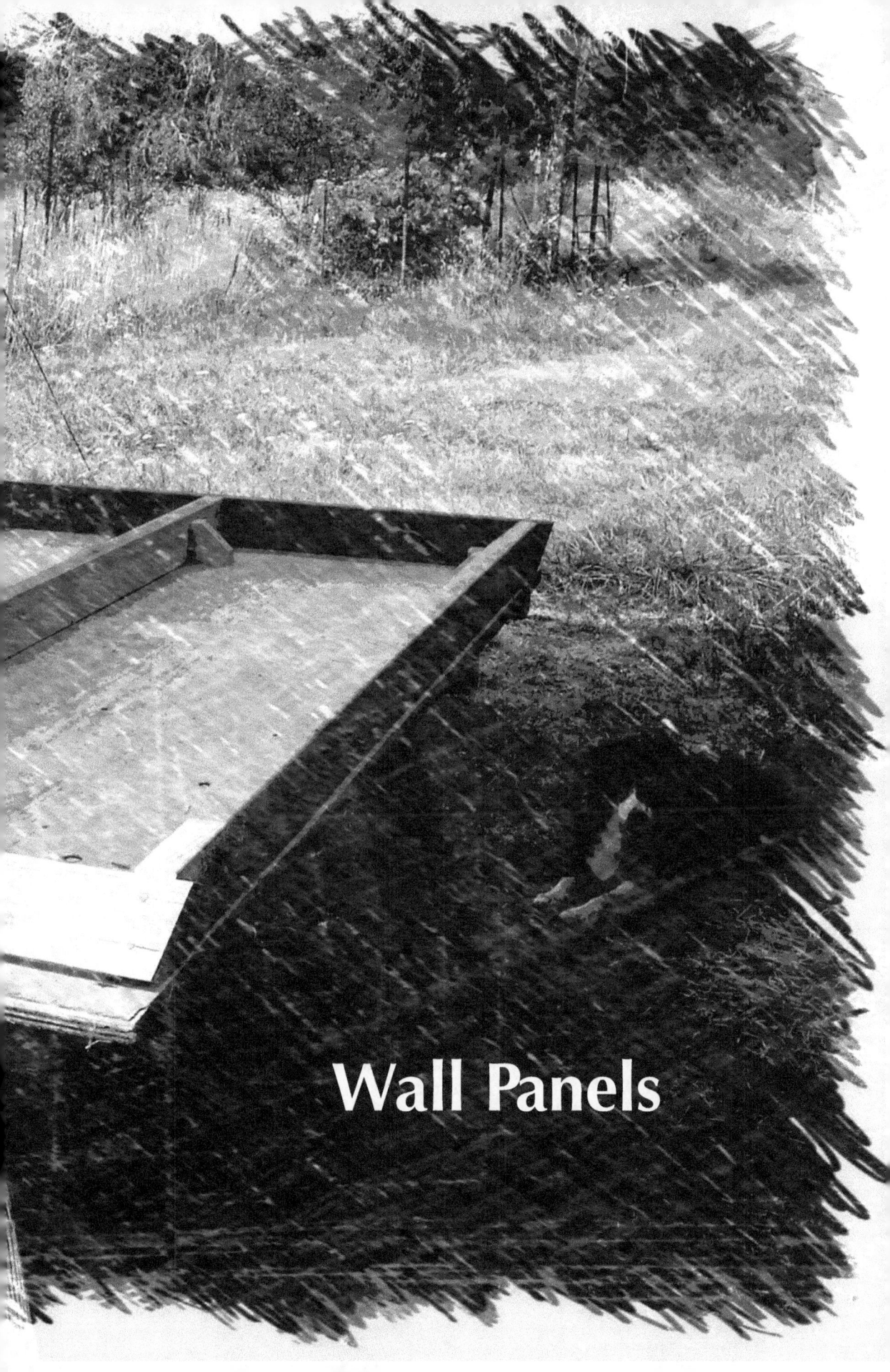

Wall Panels

Next are the 12 wall panels. Regardless of window and door placement, all of the wall panels have the same outer dimensions. The easiest and fastest method for the wall assemblies is to make a jig.

Create a stable platform at a comfortable height for the wall assembly. Set up two sawhorses and build a 2x4 frame. Screw the cross pieces to the bottom pieces so they can be easily dismantled later. Lay down a sheet of plywood and screw that down. It will be the jig base.

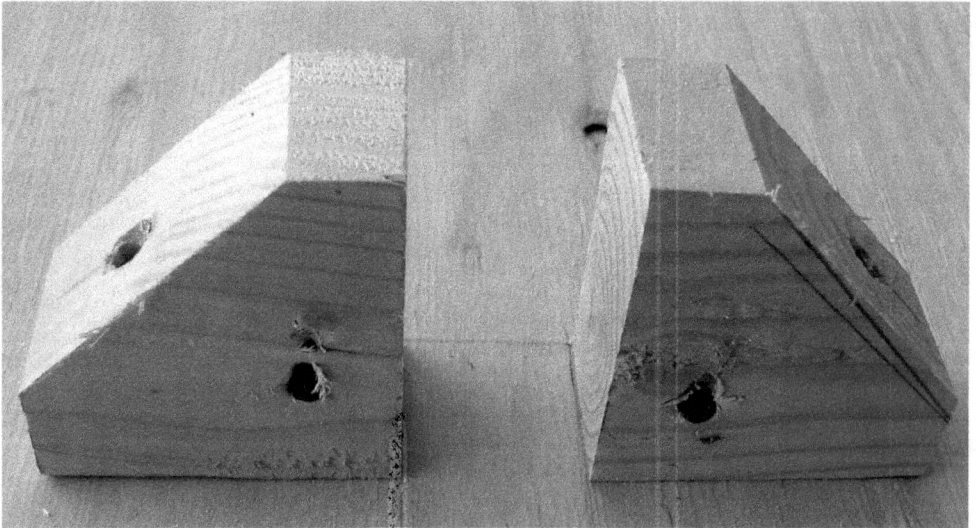

Referring to the drawing on page 40, measure and cut 8 stops for the side and middle members. Angle cut the stops so that it is easier to screw them to the plywood base. The photo shows two stops for a middle member. For a more serious set-up one could use 1-1/2" sections of 2"x2" aluminum angle material to fasten to the plywood base.

The outside stops have metal straps screwed to the bottoms, which are bent up making a base of 1-1/2" to the bend to hold the side studs in place once they are butted up against the stops.

The outer edge of the bend and therefore the stud should be 1/2" from the plywood jig edge.

Measure and cut 4 stops for the bottom member.

Mark the plywood base for wall placement, then screw in all the stops. Double-check all measurements, since you will use this jig to build all of the walls.

The members are laid in so that the side that is up is the outside of the wall. Note plate-angles go inward from above and the studs have the tops sloping, so the low side edge is up facing you. Now that the jig is complete, lay in the first set of five wall members. Use a layout stick for placing the top and bottom members correctly. It should be the same length as the long edge of the wall top and bottom.

Use the layout stick to line up the bottom member to the center by making it flush with either side. Lining it up with the center member assures that the bottom is located correctly. Mark the center and 3/4″ on either side. Nail it to the center member.

A mark on each end of the layout stick will also indicate where the plywood for the walls lines up.

THESE EDGES
SHOULD BE FLUSH

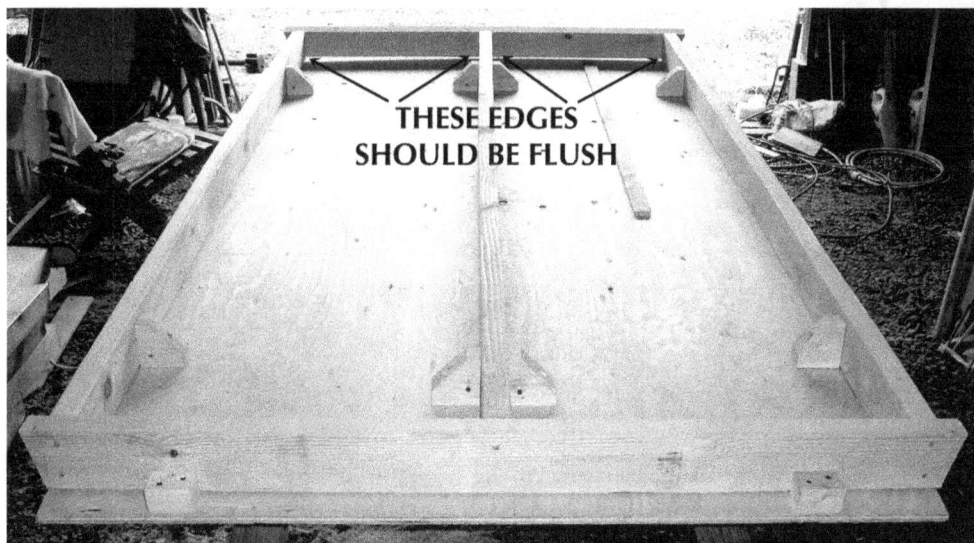

Nail the wall pieces to the bottom and top. Make sure the bottom edges are flush with each other. Use the same procedure for the top member. Before nailing, make sure the underside edge of the top plate member is flush with the bottom edge of the studs.

Lay a sheet of plywood on the framing members 1/2 the depth of the top plate (or 3/4″ up onto it). Line it up to your marks and screw down one corner. Check it again before starting to nail. The bottom of the plywood sheet should overlap the bottom plate by 5″. Center the sheet on the top and bottom plates.

Snap lines for nailing. The bottom and center are the most crucial since you can't see them.

Use the measuring stick and nail it off. Then it's time for the next panel. Note plywood half way into top plate in the photo.

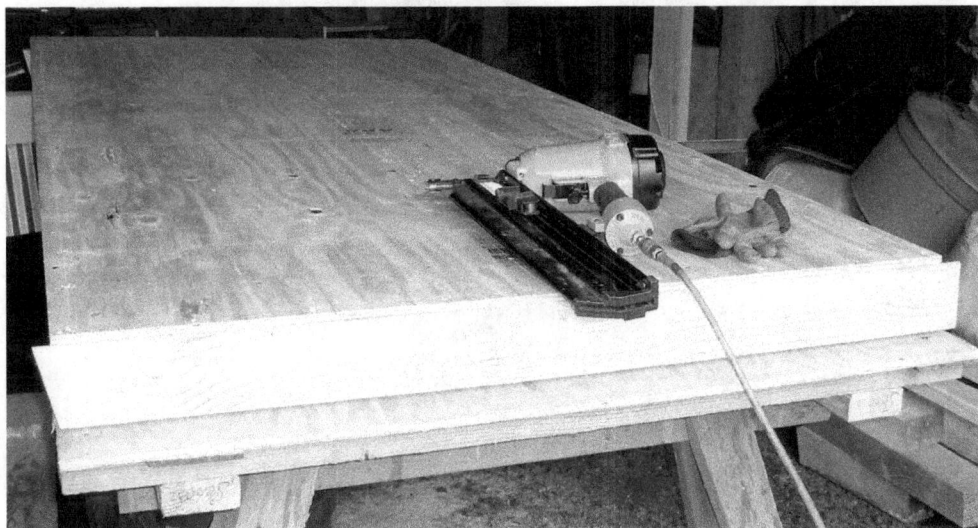

For door and window openings, just use standard framing. You can put in a
temporary center member to attach the wall members if you want.
A standard 3'x6'-8" exterior door wants 38-1/2" between the two vertical
support members. For the header height, add up the height of the door (80"),
threshold, and jam + some shim space. Be sure to consider your finished floor
height as well if applicable.

Double up the studs on each side of the door. One set supports the "header."
the other continues to the top plate.

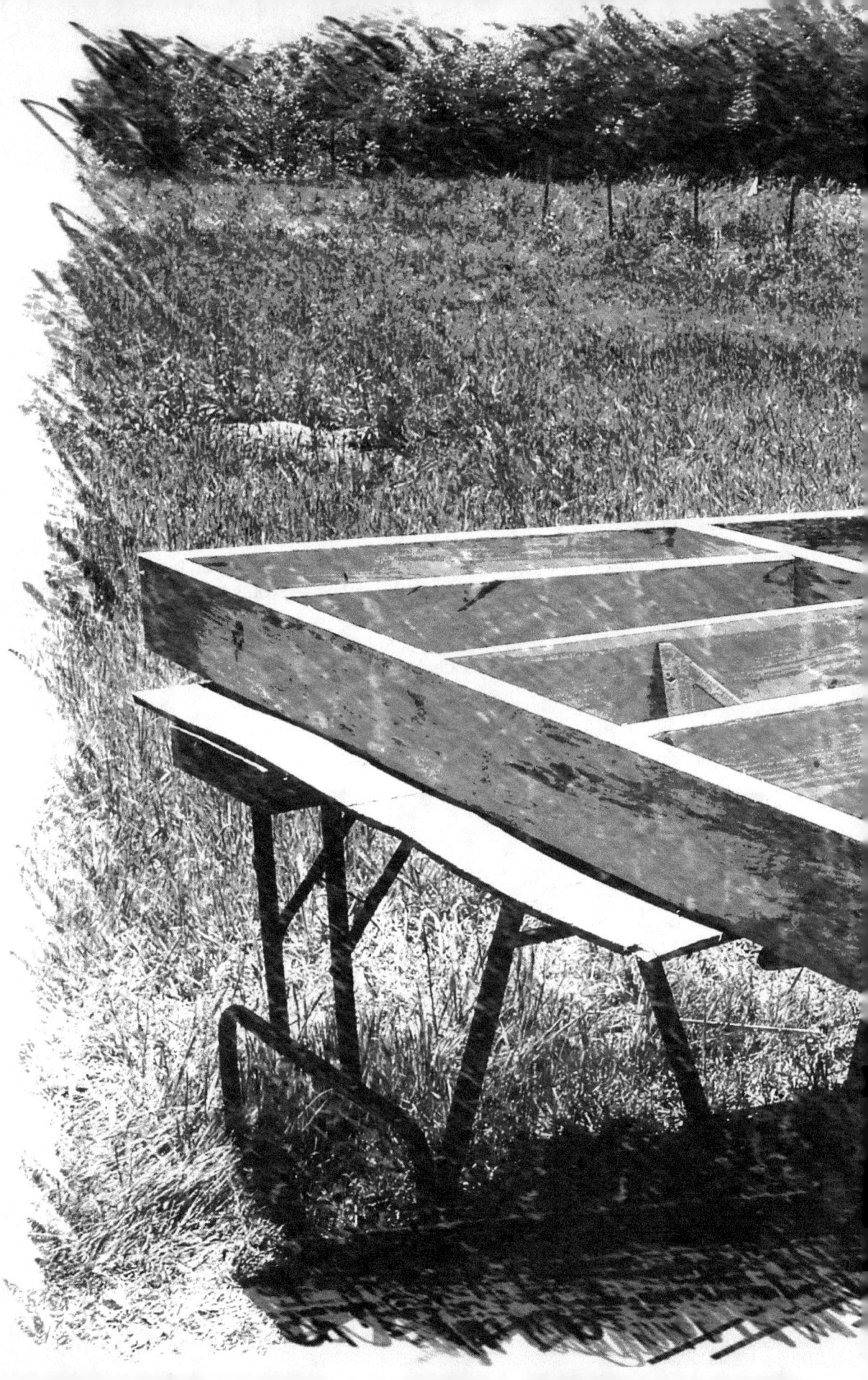

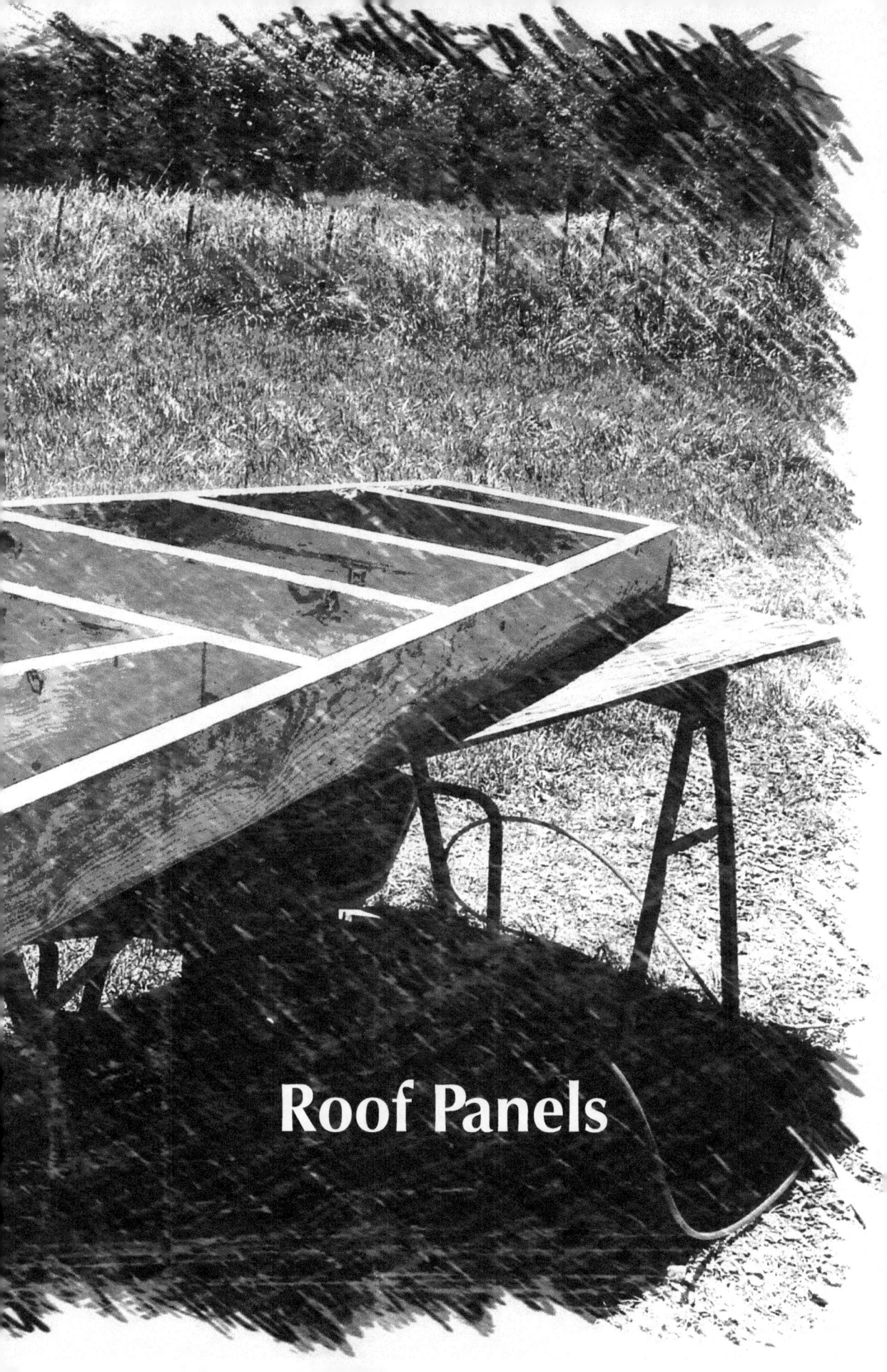

Roof Panels

The 12 roof panels are pretty straight-forward as far as assembly. Position the four perimeter members - the two sides, the shortest (top), and the longest (bottom) on the work table. Referring to the roof panel drawing on page 42 for the dimensions, make your layout guide. These are your "long point" dimensions which are easier to see when nailing together interior to side members.

Using the layout guide, mark for long points on the interior of the side perimeter members. Square down that mark. Hold interior pieces in place and nail, making sure not to force the sides out (bowing). Set in the tail end pieces which create the eaves. All tail end members are square cut on both ends. Use the layout guide to mark edges and square down. Nail in members. The assembly is ready for the plywood sheathing and should look like the photos shown here.

Use the layout guide you made to postion the interior members correctly. Be careful not to bow out the sides. Slide member downward to maintain straight.

Lay out the plywood so you get the best use out of it for each panel.

We recorded a movie of the entire assembly. See information about the videos in the Resources at the end of this book.

Jigs make the measuring process easier and more accurate. There are many measurements that would be necessary and pulling out the tape would be tedious and a potential cause for errors. Here are four layout sticks to help simplify your measuring.

A. This layout stick has the measurements for the overall width of the wall panel, plus the center. Also, the stick is the width of framing with marks (notchout) for where the plywood lands inside of the overall width for centering the plywood on wall panel framing (top & bottom plates). It also has a 6" on center nailing pattern. You can add whatever makes your work easier.

B. This layout stick is for the nailing pattern. I placed the nails in a pattern of every 6" on all the edges, 6" interior. Since I was using a nail gun, I simply laid the guide down next to where I was nailing and nailed next to the marks on the stick.

C. This layout stick has marks for drilling the holes for the roof spikes/screws that hold the panel to the rafters. Starting at about 6" in from each end, I divided the rest into about 20" increments. At the top I put marks L/R for left or right sides of the panel and TOP. Always positioning top to the same end of the panel, L guides the marks to the left, R to the right. By aligning the center of L with the top edge of the panel on one side and (the center of R) on the opposite side assures that spikes don't coinside/collide when nailing the panel down next to each other.

D. This layout stick is used to predrill the holes for the spikes or screws that fasten the roof. If the roof panel is 2x6 use 14° angle, if 2x4 use 21° to cut your tapered block. With this angle you should be drilling into the framing about 1/4" from its "inside" edge and exiting at the bottom about 1/4" from its "outside" edge.

Mark and prestart your hole prior, to cut down on wear on your guide. Mark the top of the guide with a bold black centerline and the drill line down the face where the bit will ride as a visual to help you work. The tail provides for screwing the guide in perpendicular...no hands needed.

Lay out the panel for the "spike" hole spacing, using your drilling jig to mark for distance into the panel.

Then make a small pre-drill into the marked spot. This prevents the bit from drifting when you tilt it at an angle against your drilling jig.

So here is the objective: the spike would ideally enter the roof panel framing at a point just inside the inner edge of the 2x6 or 2x4 say 1-3/8" over from the outer edge and exiting at a point that is at the outer (lower) edge of the 2x6 or 2x4 over from its inner edge.

Thus a tilt angle of (2x6) 14° or (2x4) 21-1/2° . So you should feel the tip of a spike poked through your hole somewhere close to the edge of the framing.

Using the layout guide, mark where holes, for spikes to be driven later, will be drilled. The layout guide is set up so there is a left and a right (L/R) marking at the top - offset by 3/4". Use it consistently, (L) left to the left side of the panel, and (R) right to the right. This is done so that spikes from adjacent panels when installed do not collide with each other in the beam rafter.

The drilling jig has a tail on it so that it can be fastened to the roof panel with a single screw. Make sure that the screw won't be in the path of the drill bit coming by, i.e. offset it from the centerline.

Once mounted, the guide will keep you close to the desired angle and at a fairly close vertical. Once you drill through you can check for accuracy.

Flip the panel over and add insulation. I used R21 fiberglass, but rigid would work well, too. Cut and fit OSB or plywood, and the panel is complete.

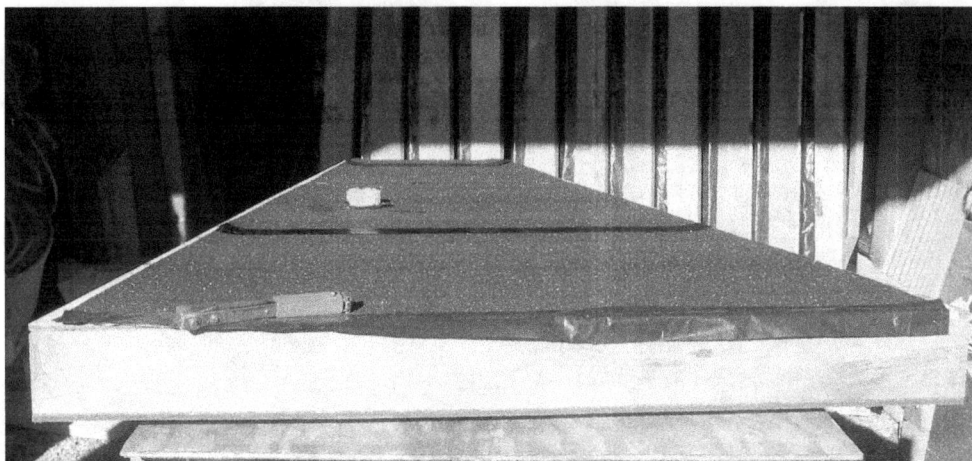

You can also add roofing material at this point. The underlayerment here is ice and snow shield. It's not cheap, but works here better than felt or anything else I've used and holds up well for a long time.

The roofing material is left away from the edges to allow access to the nail holes where nails/screws will be driven to fasten the panel to the beam rafters.

The Rafters

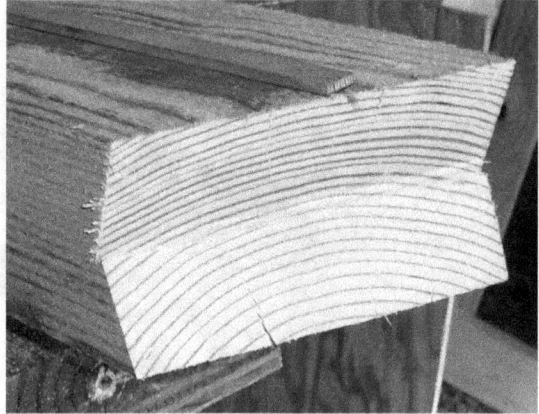

The rafters in this yurt were custom-milled 3x5 Douglas fir. In the materials list, the rafters are the 4x6s you'll acquire from a lumberyard, which are 3-1/2"x5-1/2" if you weren't aware. Regardless, the same methods need to be employed to prep the rafters for final installation.

Refer to the drawing on page 47. The top cut on the rafter is made by two inward cut compound angles - made up of the 4-1/2" in 12" slope and the 15 degree angle to make up a 12-sided polygon. This insures that the rafter meets snugly up with the ring.

Set saw blade for half the beam rafter thickness. Layout plumb cut on both sides. Cut half way through from each face. Cut the angles at the top first, as it is the critical fit. If you need to adjust you have plenty to work with.

Then repeat at the rafter tail. Only now the cuts form an outward projection. While this isn't necessary, as the facia could cover the exposed "ears" if left a square cut, it looks and is more finished. There are other details one can do to the tails: level cuts to minimize the tip of the tail, or rounded ends like a fiddle

The rafter attaches to the ring and spans overhead, landing on the wall, and continues to create an overhang. The cable that runs through each rafter goes through a hole drilled at 1/2 the height of the rafter or centerline of the height. And the cable will be positioned just inside of the exterior wall line projected upward.

Using a measuring stick, measure down the rafter, starting from the plumb cut (position your measuring stick midway on the plumb) the correct distance to the cable hole on the centerline of the rafter height, positioned just inside of the exterior face of the wall (refer to the drawing).

Drill a 11/16" hole using a paddle bit. Drill approximately half way through from one side, flip the beam over. Check for accuracy by squaring around the beam. Make marks and drill the last half way meeting the previous hole from the other side. Clean out and check to see if the sleeve will fit through.

Apply glue to a precut metal cable sleeve (1/2" electrical conduit piece) and smear some into the hole. Insert the cable sleeve and seat it into place.

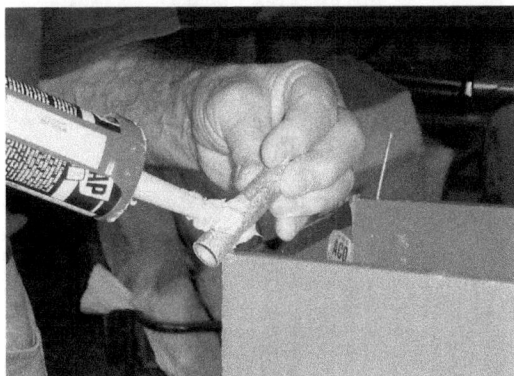

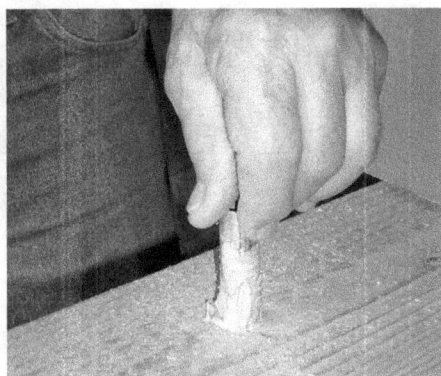

Drill holes for the bolt, washers and nut. A double hole provides enough room to get the components into place and to tighten with a socket wrench. The paddle bit allows you to drill at steep angles because the center point is long.

Drill the first hole closest to the end of the rafter. This end fits against the ring framing. Drill this hole 1″ to 1-1/8″ deep. The hole is tilted to a 4-1/2″/12 angle (matching the roof slope).

Drill the second hole 1″ (center to center - see image) away down the rafter towards the tail end. Drill until bottom is planing out (flush) with the first hole.

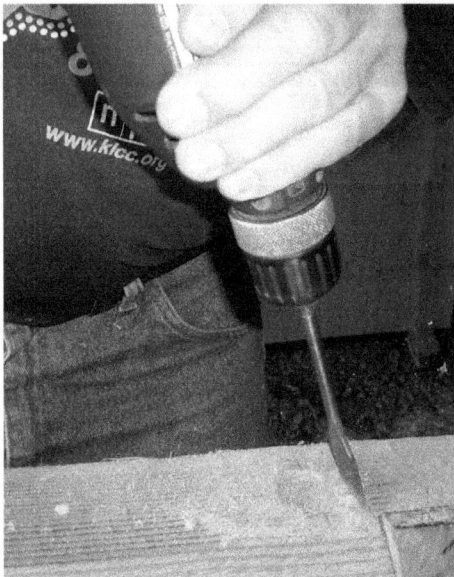

FLUSH

Next is drilling the hole for the bolt to attach the rafter to the ring. Measure from the bottom of the rafter up 2-3/8" in the center of the "V" looking cut. Draw a perpendicular line from the mark to the side of the rafter. Square across from the mark to locate where the ring-rafter bolt will come through. The goal is to drill straight through to the center of the top of the rafter.

Make a cardboard guide of a 20-1/2 degree angle (4-1/2/12 translated to degrees). This will be a right triangle where the short leg is the plumb cut of the rafter; the next leg, perpendicular to the plumb cut, is perpendicular is the line up of the hole to be drilled and the sloped leg is the roof plane. Tape to the top of the rafter.

Make a sighting guide stick that extends about 8" past the rafter on either end. Make cardboard tabs that are the distance from the top to the hole location MINUS 1/2 of the thickness of the drill bit.

Tape them to the sighting guide stick. This will help you to keep the drill bit at the correct tilt. Clamp the guide stick to the top of the rafter. The guide stick is your aiming device along side the cardboard guides.

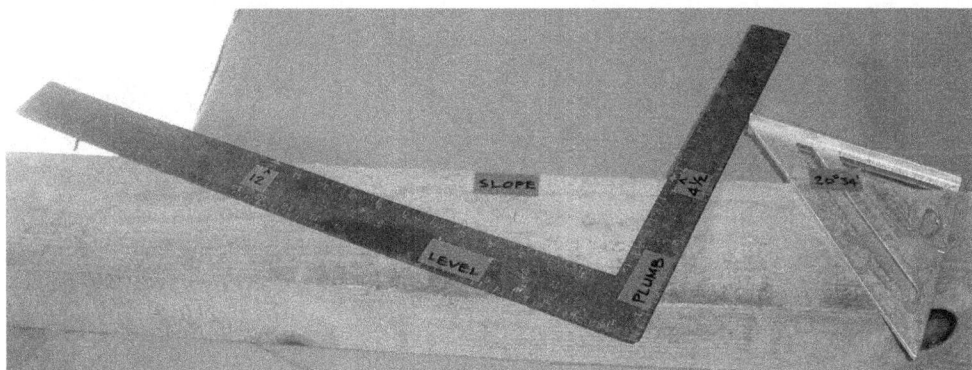

Use the smaller of the long-shank high-speed drill bits to create the hole. This allows for minor mistakes without routing out a huge hole that will create a bad fit for the bolt. You want a snug, accurate fit.

Predrill a small hole on either side to get started and mark the long shank at half the distance of the complete hole. Then sight down the tabs and drill half the distance of the total bolt hole.

Repeat the process of drilling half way through from each end. Once the holes meet, bore all the way through.

When the hole seems clear and straight, go back in with the larger 3/8″ long-shank high-speed bit, being careful to stay in the first hole and making sure the bolt can go through, and again, bored all the way through.

This process is not always easy, and practicing on a mock-up is a good idea. An accurate job assures that the bolt comes through at the exact center of the rafter. That way, the bolt is out of the way of the roof panel that sets on top. A video showing the entire process is in the Resources at the end of the book.

Once prepared, the rafters can be sanded and stained or painted. Don't forget that they will be visible from the interior of the yurt, adding to the building's unique look.

The Tower
and the Ring

The Tower

Refer to the drawing on page 48. The tower is designed to be the correct height to hold the ring in place until the rafters and cables, then roof panels are installed.

I built my tower so that it broke apart into two pieces making it easy to haul to the yurt site for final assembly. Plus, it otherwise would not have fit through the doorway. To note, my tower is for a 6-foot ring; the drawing is for a 3-foot ring.

The Rings

The ring not only supports the skylight dome, it is an integral part of the yurt structure. My yurt has a 6-foot dome and ring assembly. The yurt described in the material list uses a 3-foot dome. Directions for it will follow.

The 12-gauge metal (roughly 1/8") to install inside the ring provides stability to the wooden structure and provides something substantial to bolt to the rafters. When the assembly was done, I had about a 200 pound ring to install in my yurt. A 3-foot ring will not be that heavy or unwieldy.

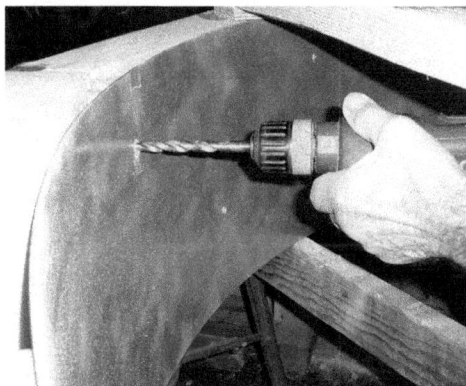

Below is the 6-foot wooden ring with metal installed and blocking in the corners before they were hammered and screwed into place

For the 3-foot dome, refer to the drawings on pgs 44-45 and start with the sky-light dome ring.

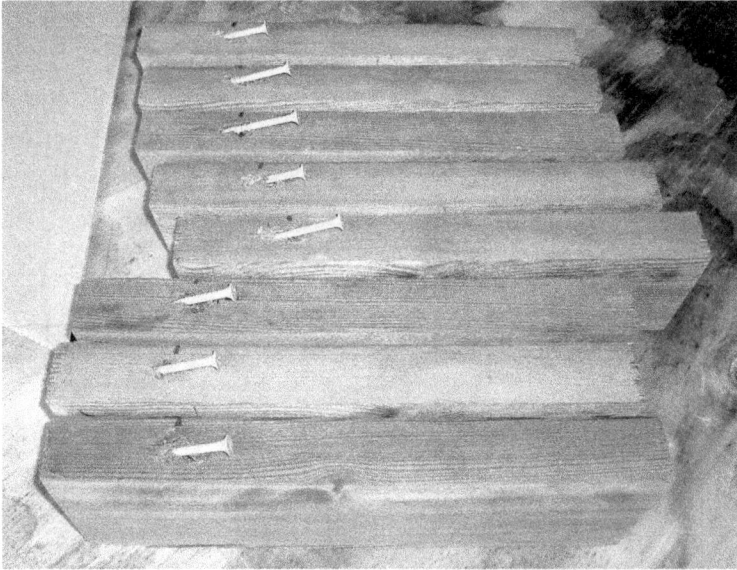

The 12 pieces that were cut from a piece of treated wood have a 15° angle (downward) on the outside edge.

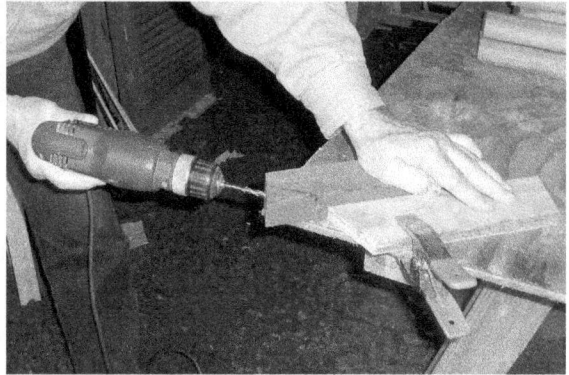

Predrill the pieces to make assembly easier.

Assemble the pieces. Note the slope from interior to outer edge goes down.

Screw the segments of the skylight base together.

Two crossing pieces help stabilize the "ring" and also elevate it while doing the remaining steps.

Top up and resting on its stabilizers, the ring is ready for the flashing.

The flashing goes on in three pieces. Precut the flashing a bit longer on each segment than the ring segment length. Test fit the first cut to make sure it works and is not too long.

This is laying out for the precut.

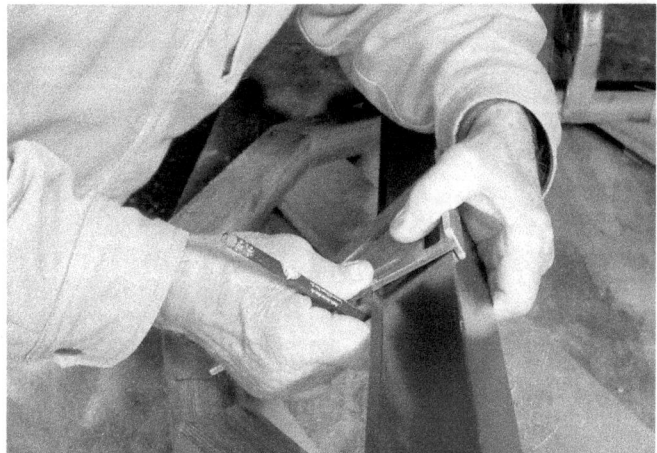

Wrap flashing pieces around, getting corners to align.

Overlap at
a corner
shown here.

Once the flash-
ing pieces are
all around and
overlapping
each other at
the ends, and
all corners align
well, clamp
them all into
place.

Drill a hole in
the overlap at
each corner.

I used copper nails to fasten the corners down. Be sure to put some caulk under the lap joint before hammering down. I use Flex-Seal as shown on the materials list.

Cut another cap piece to put over each lap joint for further water penetration prevention. Use caulk to secure the cap piece.

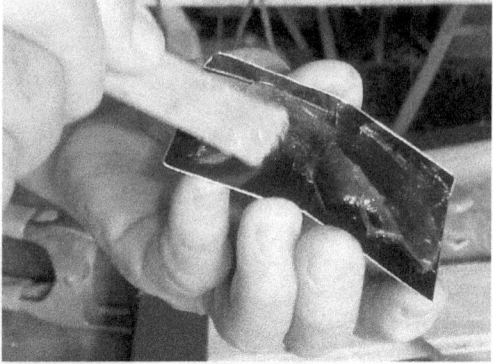

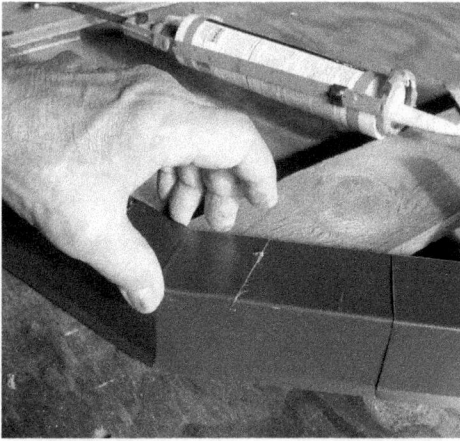

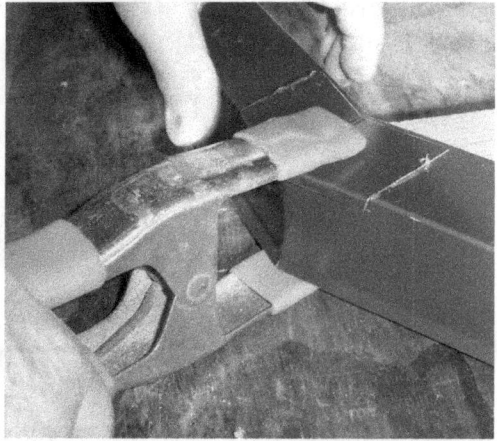

The cap piece of flashing helps to prevents water from seeping into the joints. Clamp the caps in place until the caulk sets up a bit.

Note: the flashing leg going down needs to be long enough to go about 1-1/2" down over the rafter beam ring assembly so that screws can be used to attach to the ring assembly. The leg should be 3" deep to be able to connect to the beam ring assembly.

After the corner caps have been placed and sealed dry, the skylight dome is ready to be placed upon it. Line the bottom edge of the skylight with foam water-barrier tape. Single sided sticky is sufficient, and can be placed on either the skylight or the base. The skylight is easier.

To fit the skylight, it needs to be cut so that it has 12 sides. The easiest way to lay this out is to use a large sheet of cardboard - 2 pieces taped together can work. The "light" portion of the skylight is 36" and the flange is 2". Thus, draw a circle with a diameter of 40" - 20" radius. Divide this circle in half, then that in half. You will have four quarters. Each quarter is divided into thirds: 90° / 3 gives 30°.

Once the circle is divided, all of the divisions intersect the drawn 40" circle. Each point is connected with a straight line to its neighbor. That gives the 12 sides. That portion to the outside is cut off. Lay the skylight over your template. Mark where to cut. It helps if you cut the skylight just slightly under the base dimension. It's preferable the skylight doesn't overhang the base.

The plexiglass cuts easily with a sharp wood-cutting saw. Be careful as the plastic gets a sharp edge after it is cut. Either file the edges or handle carefully.

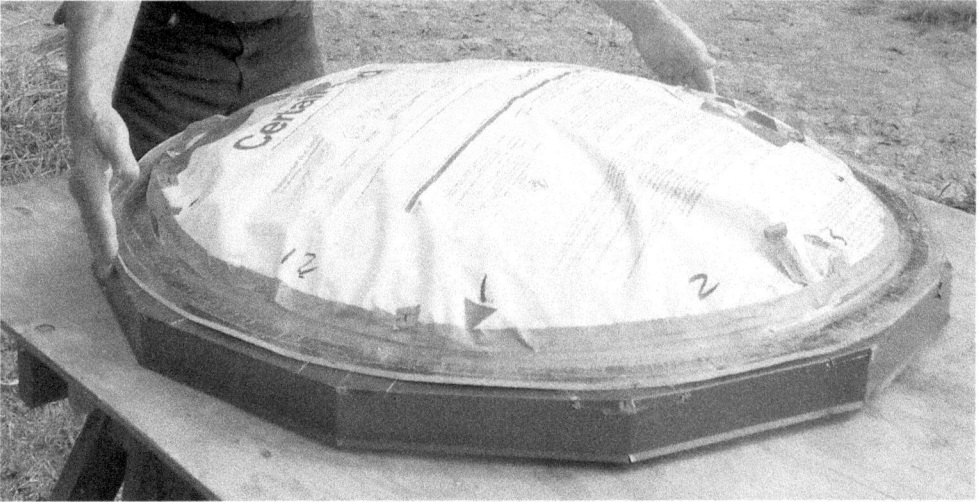

After placing the foam tape, lay the skylight dome over the base, aligning the 12 sides up.

The capping pieces have all been precut with a 15° angle at each end. They have also been pre-drilled with two holes for attachment to the base.

Place a strip of butyl along the underside of the edge that goes toward the "light" and at each angled end and on the backside of the predrilled hole.

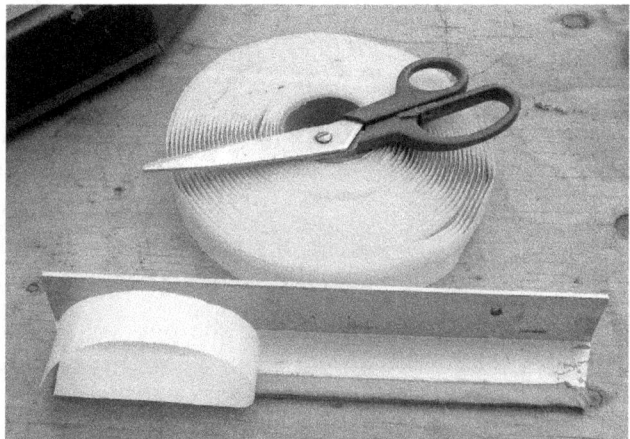

Stick a couple pieces of butyl or caulk over the screw holes to further prevent water penetration.

Fasten the capping pieces with two screws into the base, making sure the skylight and base are well pressed together and the foam tape is compressed.

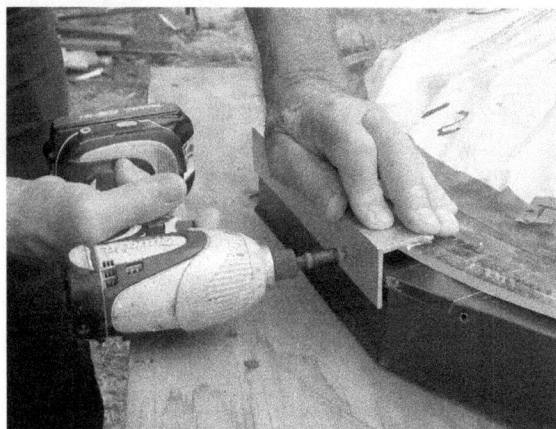

Complete the fastening of all 12 capping pieces. Check to see that butyl has sealed all of the gaps. When achieved, it should be water-tight for its lifetime.

Refer to the drawing on page 46. The rafter ring is built using a 2x12 and a 2x4, providing the width needed. Select a 2x12 with at least one good face on the side. Edge-glue a 2x4 to it and clamp until secure.

Face glue 1/2" plywood to the glued assembly, spreading it evenly.

Chalk-line for the
screws and lay the
plywood on the
glued face.

Clamp it
down, lining
up the chalk
lines.

Use an array of screws, spaced about 6" apart. These are temporary, to be removed after the glue sets.

Fasten the screws snugly to pull the plywood tight to the assembly.

When the glue is set, remove all the screws and lay out the assembly for final width, then cut.

Next, angle-cut the assembly into the 12 segment lengths as per the drawing. The plywood goes to the inside (shorter dimension)

Sand the good face and bottom edge adjacent.

Place all 12 segments into a round arrangement. Pull them together tightly with strap clamp or rope cinched tight. Pre-drill, then screw the segments together.

You can use a t-bevel to assure your angles are staying on mark as you begin.

Use a clamp to keep the segments from sliping up and down, clamping right on the joint. Check the angle as you predrill the holes.

Once it's all screwed together, drill the hole for the rafter/beam bolt. When the metal ring gets inserted inside, then you'll back drill through this hole into and through the metal ring. Doing it this way makes sure the hole is properly aligned.

Check for "roundness" or equal diagonals and put on some temporary ties to hold it in place. If necessary, use a bar clamp to pull overly "long" diagonals, then put on framework for the tower.

I used 1/2″ plywood for the first layer of framework that attaches the ring to the tower. The tower attaches to the bottom of the ring - the part you sanded. It will butt against the plywood layer and screw to the second layer - the 2x4.

The second layer is screwed in perpendicular to the first.

The 12 gauge metal ring will be a bear to work with, but it can be done. Bend the end with a slight offset (for overlapping) for the interior of the skylite assembly.

After the end is bent, clean the metal and sand it, even paint it if you want. It will be visible from inside the yurt.

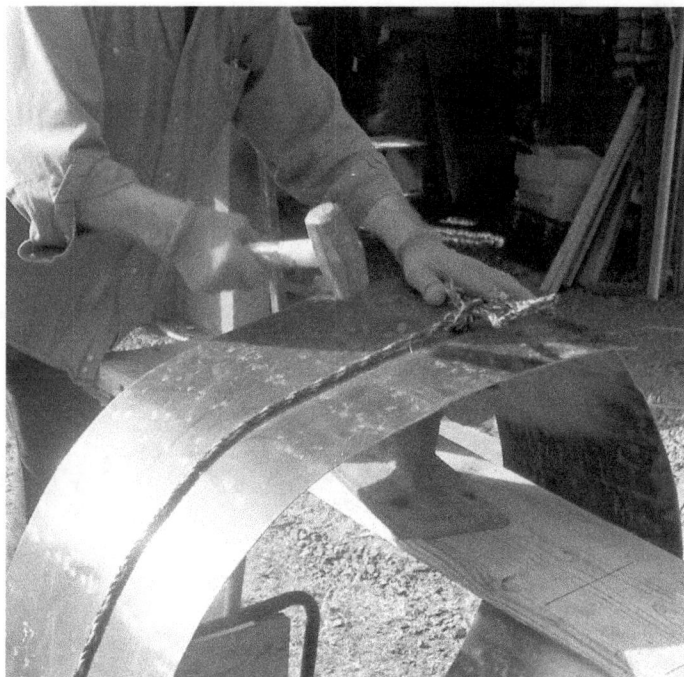

Bending a 14″ wide 12 gauge 10′ long piece of steel plate was a bit more of a challenge than I had thought it would be.

The radius is about 18″ and devising a good work surface was part of the challenge. I couldn't "pull" it round by using ropes around it, as clamps, and pulling tight.

A great deal of pounding with a 2 lb. sledge finally got it to yield. But I still wasn't happy with the results.

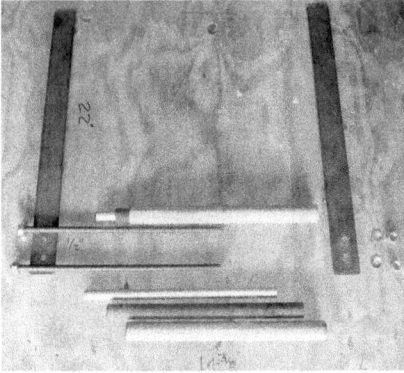

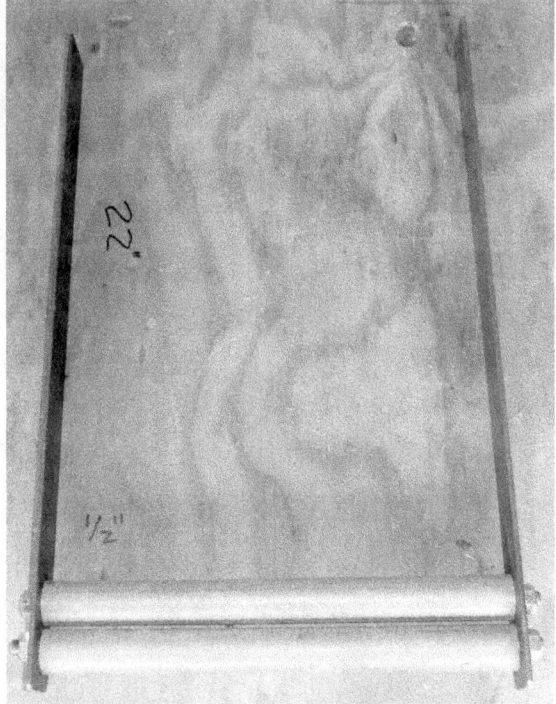

So, I made this bending gadget. The two sides are 2″ wide x 3/ 6″ plate, drilled with (2) 1/2″ holes. Two 1/2″ all thread rods about 16″ long hold a series of increasingly larger diameter pipes. Starting with 1/2″ conduit up to 1-1/2″ o.d. pipe; washers and nuts hold it all secure.

To use the gadget: slide it down the ring metal (between the pipe rollers). I think I started in the middle of the ring metal and worked out to each end.

Make your bends fairly close together and not very much - a slight bend.

Unfortunately, the gadget leaves creases at each bend. I pounded on it afterward to smooth the creases out a bit and to get a hammered look. It will be rustic!

There is always the option to have this part made by a metal manufacturer. If you go that route, make sure the dimensions you give them will fit snug inside your wood ring structure. Total of all your interior wall to wall (perpendicular) 12 sides, then average six dimensions. Half of that is outer radius of the ring.

Once the metal ring was bent round, it was placed inside of the wooden ring. The metal ring had been predrilled (12 holes) for attachment. I placed a tight band round the wood ring to assure against bulging out. The holes were aligned with the center lines of each of the wood segments. Start on the side opposite the loose metal ends. Clamp and squeeze to get proper alignment.

Once you get to the loose ends of the metal, clamp to align the last two holes at either side, then fasten them. Drill through the overlap holes to secure the metal to itself and the wood ring.

Screw #10 x 1-1/2" length screws through the predrilled holes.

15°   150°   15°
75°
30°
THE CENTERLINE OF
SQUARED CARDBOARD
SHEET ACTS AS A BI-
SECTION OF ANGLE.

LAYOUT AND
CUT AWAY
UPPER PART.

THE TURN OF ONE
FACE RELATIVE TO
THE NEXT FACE
ON THE RING.

DRILLBIT
SIGHTLINE
MARK BOLD

STIFF CARDBOARD   10"

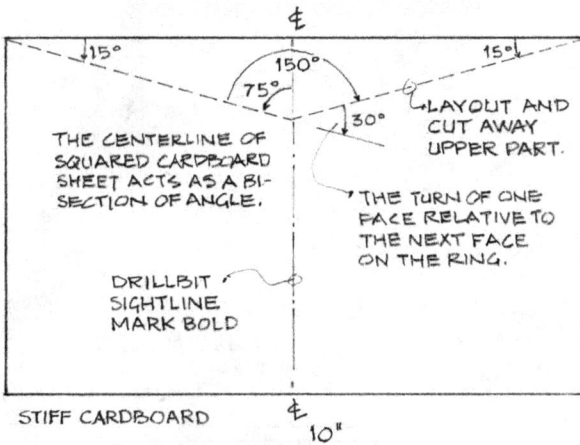

When drilling the holes for the rafter bolts, it is important that the holes radi-
ate straight out from the ring center. That is difficult to set up, so make a drilling guide by cutting out a piece of cardboard 6"x10" and follow the drawing
shown.

Once the metal has been attached to the interior of the wood ring, you are
ready to make all the flashing pieces for the ring. These are being pre-made,
waiting for after the ring has been installed and all the roofing has been done.
Check the illustration below.

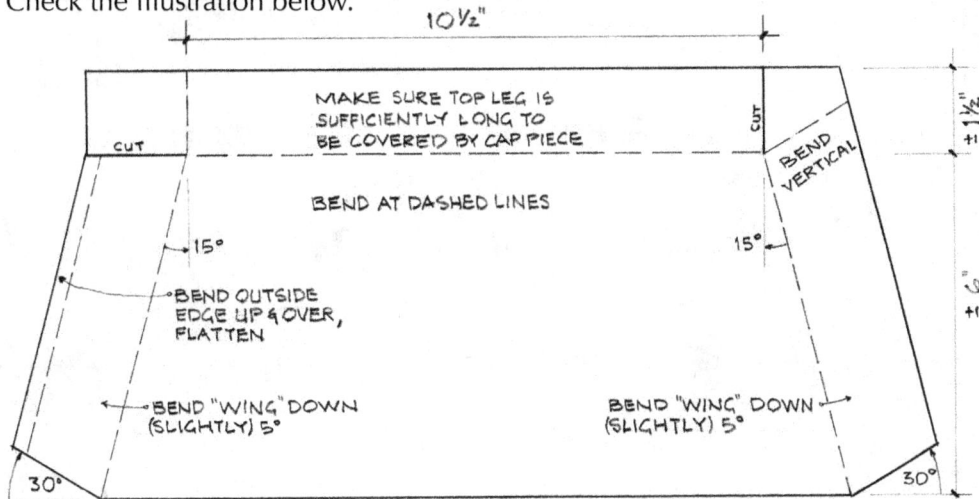

10½"

MAKE SURE TOP LEG IS
SUFFICIENTLY LONG TO
BE COVERED BY CAP PIECE

CUT   CUT   BEND VERTICAL

± 1½"

BEND AT DASHED LINES

15°   15°

BEND OUTSIDE
EDGE UP & OVER,
FLATTEN

± 6"

BEND "WING" DOWN   BEND "WING" DOWN
(SLIGHTLY) 5°   (SLIGHTLY) 5°

30°   30°

FLASHING
ENDVIEW

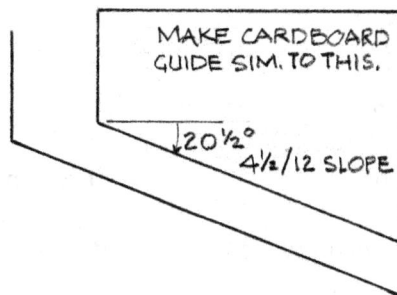

MAKE CARDBOARD
GUIDE SIM. TO THIS.

20½°
4½/12 SLOPE

Put butyl caulk at the corner and at the bottom of the vertical and over. The next flashing piece will cover over the butyl and seal it from water. Use screws or roofing nails to attach. Continue around until completed.

Once the roofing is installed, the flashing pieces will be placed just over the roofing material surface. Before the flashing goes on, you should have used Fortiflashing® at the top, over your roofing and down the sides of your rafter beam ring. Work from the lowest toward the top overlaps on top, facing downhill. Just think how water runs and make sure everything is sealed up well.

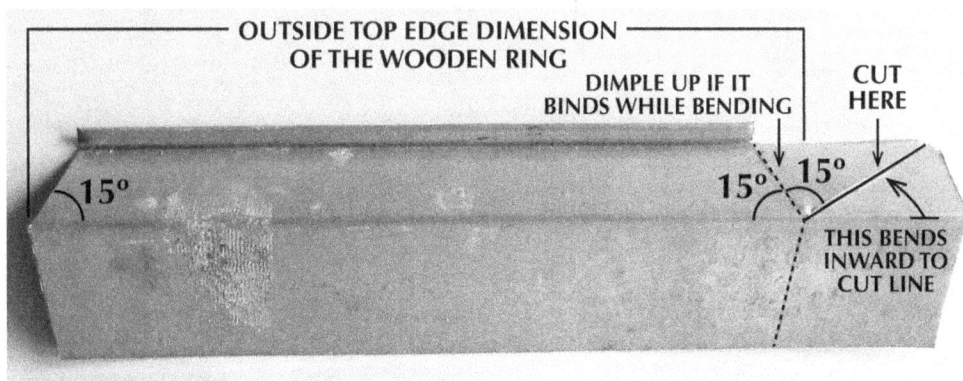

OUTSIDE TOP EDGE DIMENSION
OF THE WOODEN RING

DIMPLE UP IF IT
BINDS WHILE BENDING

CUT
HERE

15°

15° 15°

15°

THIS BENDS
INWARD TO
CUT LINE

For the cap flashing, use the dimensions (length) of your wood segments of your ring. Make flashing pieces as in the picture out of 2x2 flashing with 1/4 kick on edge. Put kick at the top.

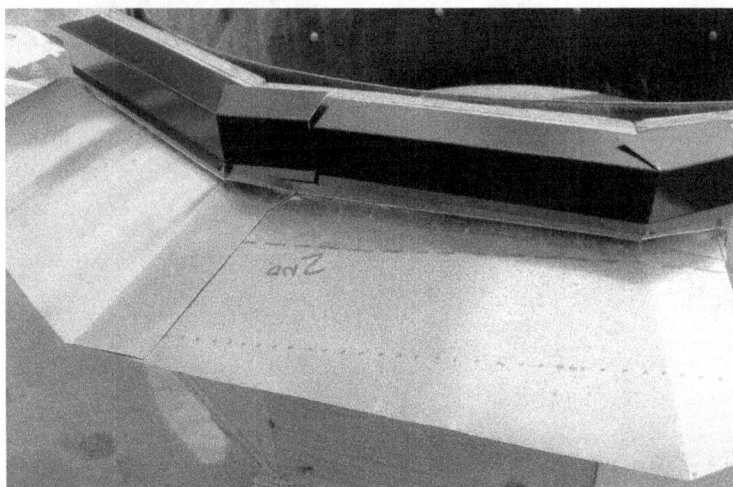

I wound up using some nicer flashing pieces that I had, but the above photo shows how you cut and bend the the pieces.

The photo below shows the flashing on my 6-foot ring, done in a similar fashion.

The Yurt Assembly

Floor Panels

Before beginning floor panel installation, check one more time that the foundation beams are at the appropriate distance to the corners, and that the center pedestal is level to the height of the beams.

Once everything is checked out and shimmed if necessary, cut and fit plastic sheeting on the ground under the yurt. It's a lot easier to do this now than later. Then install a tie from one side to the other across the center. Screw down the tie to lock the beams tight to the center and to each other.

Start with the first floor panel in any beam segment (they should all be the same). If you have rough terrain to deal with, think about how you can avoid stumbling around by sliding floor panels across previously placed panels.

Also, because there is an overlapping plywood edge, you will always travel around the structure placing the panel edge to overlay the last panel locked down.

Put a screw in the panel through to the pedestal after determining that the placement is "centered" to the center and flush at the beams.

Place two screws near each corner into the beam.

Continue the process until complete. Place a second screw at the center, into the pedestal. In this photo you can see my pedestal is a bit more involved than what you will build. That's because I was reusing footing piers from another project.

When you get to the last panel, it may turn out that the edge needs adjusting in order for it to fit in. Trim off what is necessary and stuff it in.

Once all the floor panels are down and fastened, it will look something like this. Now's a good time to take a break before the next step. Installing the floor panels took two old boys about an hour.

Fill the center cavity with insulation cut to fit snug. I used rigid 3″ and then spray foam for the remaining spaces. Then, build a 12-sided cover out of 5/8″ plywood and screw it down.

Because the rainy season was looming, I covered the floor panels with ice and snow shield. I allowed 3″ overlays and heated with a solder torch for a good seal since it was too cold to properly seal otherwise.

The ice and snow shield wouldn't wrap down over the floor edges, so I cut it flush with the floor edge, leaving a strip of the tackiness protection intact. Then I cut a piece of 6 mil plastic sheeting to lap over the floor panel by about 3″ and drape down the panel depth. I removed the protection strip on the shield and bonded it to the plastic, creating a continuous water barrier.

Wall Panels

Stack the wall panels in a convenient location. Place them in separate solid wall pile and window/door pile to ease selection. Mark on the floor where the window and door panels go. Now you are ready to place the wall panels. You can start wherever you want, and the direction you go isn't important this time.

Stand up the first wall and fasten through the wall tab that overlaps the floor panel using two of the five 1-1/2" #10 coated screws.

Then put one of the four 3" #10 coated screws through the wall panel bottom plate, near the outer studs at each corner. Keep them within the first 1-1/2" in from the plywood sheathing, thereby hitting the 2x8 framing at the outer edge of the floor panel below.

Put in all the remaining screws after all the wall panels are up and where you want them, spacing them evenly apart.

The last wall panel has to be placed from the outside, stood in vertically. Once all the walls are stood and fastened to the floor, they can be fastened to each other more securely with screws. Screws allow for adjustments later if needed.

If you stop at this point, as we did, you might want to tie a rope around the walls until you get back to it. A high wind could possibly cause issues if the structure isn't stabilized by the cable.

Wall blocks can be placed between wall panels as they are being raised by dropping them in near the top as the wall is tilted into position or set in with wall panels separated appropriately.

I find it easier to raise all of the walls and then notch the plywood away at the location of one of the two blocks. You could pre-notch in the wall panel construction phase.

Put the blocks in, spaced so that there are equal spaces between top to block, block to block. This will make insulating with rigid insulation simple.

Bring the block foward so that the space between the two framed walls is even top to bottom. Put three #12-3" screws in from each side into block.

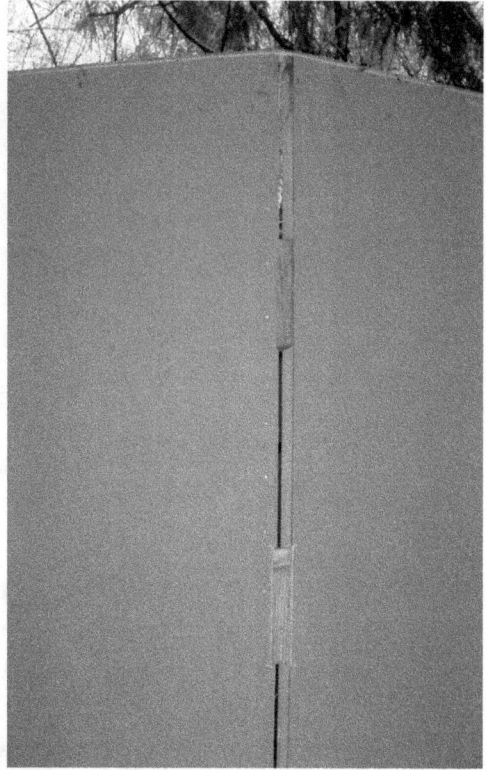

Fill in all the bits and cut out the excess plywood at this point if needed.

In preparation for the rafter beam installation you will have to flatten the corners where the wall panels meet at the top. Cut a marking tool similar to the one shown that I cut out of metal flashing. You can also use heavy cardboard from something like a cereal box.

The side markings indicate where the rafter bracket will be placed. Mark the beam rafter edges after lining up with the center of the wall meeting. The hole is a peek at your alignment.

Use the marking tool's edge to check how much you need to cut.

Use a sawzall with a sharp blade (I use a tree limbing blade) and slice off between the side markings. Use marking jig again to indicate when it is relatively flat across. Do this for all twelve corners before installing the cable.

Wall Cable

Have ready your 3/8" cable with one end swagged with a ½" turnbuckle attached in the eye. Also have ready the three 3/8" cable clamps and the 3/8" thimble. Extend the turnbuckle out as far as it will go with three or so threads showing.

Fasten the turnbuckle on a chosen wall top. A nail through the bolt eye will work. With the turnbuckle secured, lay the cable around the walls just inside on the floor of the yurt.

Move around the walls, pulling the cable up to the wall corners. Place a nail just below the cable to help support and prevent it from falling down. The cable will fit just above the top of the wall plywood and below the top of the tilted top of the top plate. Use clamps if you're a one-person operator.

Continue around until you come to the turnbuckle.

Pry the thimble apart a bit and put it through the remaining bolt eye. Run the loose end of the cable through the thimble in the eyebolt. Work all of the slack out of the cable as well as you can with someone holding while you pull alternately around.

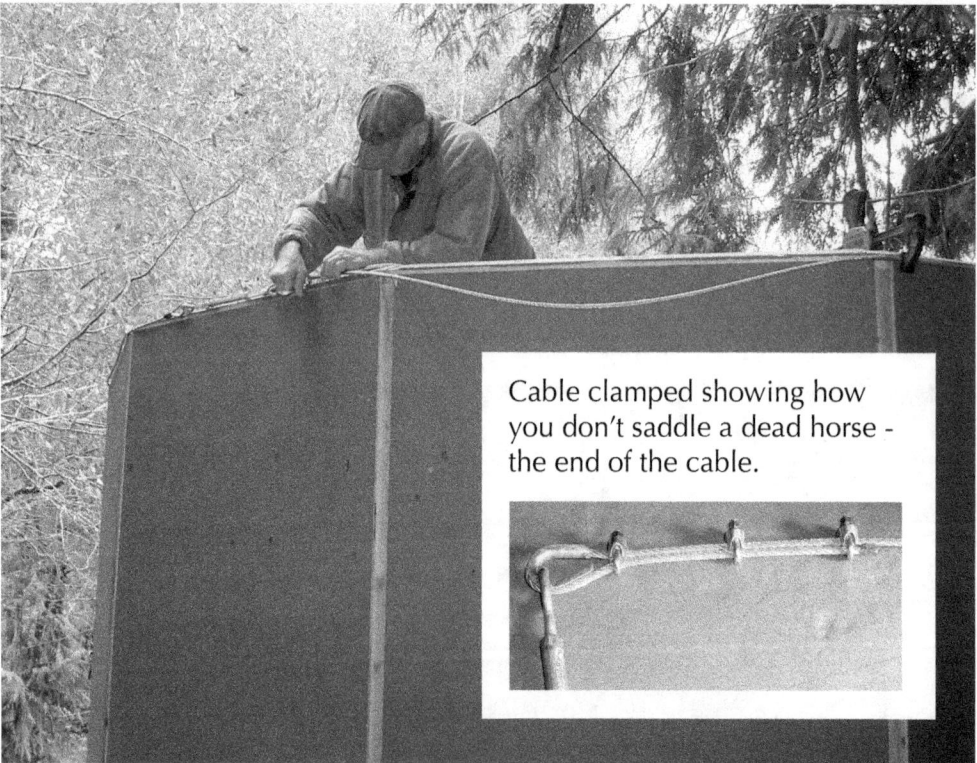

Cable clamped showing how you don't saddle a dead horse - the end of the cable.

Pull that slack through the eye. The slack end of the cable should have a minimum length of 12". Place the first cable clamp close to this cutoff end 10-11" distance from the thimble. Place the 2nd clamp as close to the thimble as possible, leaving no slack between cables. The last clamp is centered between the two. Tighten the nuts on the clamps as you proceed to the last one. Finally tighten each of the clamp nuts to 45 foot-pounds/foot torque. You will need to use a torque wrench. A mechanic will have one. Or else crank on it so that it feels like dragging.

I had the eye installed to the cable by a cable rigging company, but you can make your own just by looping the cable around the eye and fastening with three cable clamps. Make sure you don't saddle the dead horse, in other words, the base of the clamp (saddle) is placed on the live end of the cable, not the dead (loose) end.

Tighten the cable until it is really snug. The wall tops may creak a bit before it is tight. If you sprayed a little oil on the threads and it turned fairly easily you will be able to tell when it is tight. It will be very difficult to turn the turnbuckle any more. Tap the cable just off the side of the turnbuckle and you can probably feel how taunt it is. The yurt is ready for the ring tower.

Tower and Ring

First I needed to finish assembling the tower and then attach it to the ring. The ring has a frame (as shown in the second photo below) that matches up to the top of the tower corners. I just need to screw it together. The entire assembly will be hoisted up as a unit, so I don't want things coming apart.

You will notice the tower at the bottom is missing parts and the end is open.

Remember this is a 6-foot ring and the ring detailed for your yurt is 3-feet wide. Your tower and ring assembly would be done in the same manner, only you'll probably not need to go through what I did to hoist it upright. With your tower bottom cabled as shown on the next page, three people should be able to raise your assembly.

I used a strap that fastened to another strap around the ring - one strap around the ring, and ends meeting at the top end in a D-ring at the bottom end (by the floor). A strap wraps the bottom of the ring and leads up to the top end and through the aforementioned D-ring and turned out towards the truck.

A cable was run through holes drilled in the lower legs near their bottom amd fastened at the walls to prevent the tower from sliding when it was being hoisted. I also blocked it up using a house jack just to give it a head start.

The strap went up and over the doorway. I had sliced a 3-inch PVC pipe down the middle and screwed it to the top of the doorway so the strap could slide easily without binding. I hooked the end of the strap to a chain looped through tow slots on my little truck. Then I put the truck in reverse and backed up carefully. The tower had nowhere to go but up!

The ring tower rocked to a stop without issue. The next step was to get it positioned in the center of the yurt and, the corners lined up to the wall corners.

I stuck small lengths of metal conduit to get it to roll across the floor easily. The strap was employed again along with a cable winch to assist in the process.

Once the tower was roughly in place you need to line up the 12 corners of the ring to the corners of the yurt walls. This is in order for the rafters to fit properly.

The method of aligning is simple. Divide the yurt in half in two directions, each perpendicular to the other to create four equal sections. Run a string from one corner to the other side, picking a wall corner. If you built the tower correctly your strings will miss framing. Also, pick wall corners that "look" directly between the legs of the tower. Do the same with a line perpendicular wall corner to wall corner. Look at the ring. Find the closet corner over your line in one direction. Identify the other three.

Hang a plumb bob directly down from the corners. Nudge the tower until the plumb bob line "kisses" the wall corner string-lines. When you've completed this you should be centered and ready for rafter placement. Note that it helps if the bob lines are all on the same side of the wall lines clock-wise or counter-clockwise.

Rafters

Bring in the prepped rafters and set them in their respective corners.

One worker pounds in the bolts that connect the rafters to the ring while another holds the rafter on the wall to prevent it from sliding. Once all are in place, screw in the angle brackets along the walls.

The photo on the left shows the ring bolt as it emerges on the other side. It gets fastened with a washer and nut tightened with a racheting screwgun.

Above photo shows the angle bracket as I marked all the installed rafters for the blocking.

There are two methods of making the blocks for between the rafters. The first makes the blocks perpendicular to the top of the rafter (as the speed square shows), not vertically aligned with the wall plane. It tilts back at the top. This is not a compound angle. The saw blade is set at 15° and the cut is made perpendicular to the top/bottom edges.

The other method is to cut the ends of the blocks so that they fit in between the rafters with the face in the same plane as the wall. This is done by making a compound angle cut on both ends of the block. The tilt of the blade (blade angle) is 15° while the angle relative to a perpendicular line on the face of the board from top edge to bottom edge is a 5° angle. The cardboard represents a perpendicular line along its right edge.

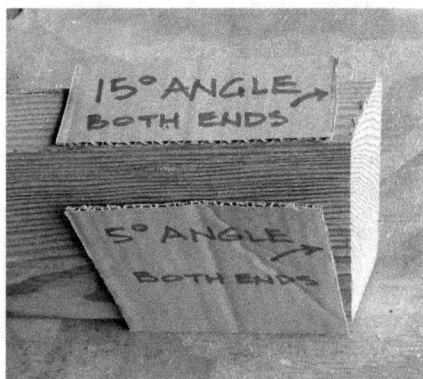

It also requires that the block's top is ripped with a 20-1/2° peak at interior (follows roof slope), and it needs to be wider. Since all of the blocks are slightly different in length - not much - they can all be precut with the angle cut on one end but left long.

I placed a support block on the face of the wall that the rafter blocks can rest on while being fastened. The rafter blocks should be placed so that the back of the block is just about in line with the inside of the wall line (stud edge). The resting block also serves as a space in or out of the end of the rafter block, keeping them even to the wall plane.

Rafter Cable

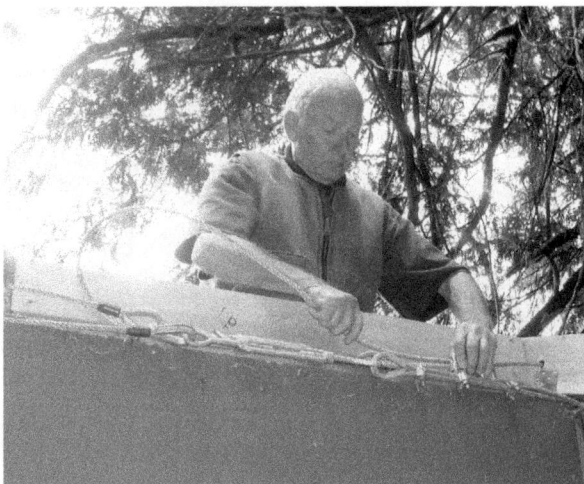

Pull the rafter cable through each of the sleeves in the rafters. Note the swaged end with thimble near my right elbow. This cable slides easily back and forth through these sleeves.

After extending the turnbuckle out as far as possible - you can still see a small portion of thread on the bolt ends in the turning body - lace the loose cable end through the turnbuckle making sure to put it in the thimble.

To save effort you can slide the three cable clips on before doing the above step. Otherwise, place cable clips one out about 10-11 inches from the turnbuckle end, another as close to the turnbuckle as possible, and the third centered between them.

Tighten nuts to about 45 ft. lbs. each. If you use a racheting screwgun it should achieve this. Leave about one foot extra length of cable past the last clip on the cable. Cut off remains. Tuck away the end.

Once the clips are tightened you can now turn the turnbuckle to tighten the cable. Turn until tight. Listen for a nice "tong" on the cable when you tap it with a bar.

Roof Panels

The time it requires to install the roof panels depends on the weight of the panels and how many good helpers you round up. The panels for this yurt, with interior sheathing, insulation, and roofing as described in the assembly, weigh roughly 120 pounds. Two old boys and three Millennials installed all 12 panels in less than two hours.

I gave everyone a run-down of what we'd be doing, explaining that it would get easier once we had a routine. I'd be up top in the ring to position and screw down each panel. The others would be muscling each panel into place and lining it up at the bottom, then hammering in the spikes.

The panels had been predrilled for spikes and screws. We also installed two handles on the bottom and one on top to make the panels less awkward to carry and position. I also made a little cart to roll them to the scaffolding.

Once the first panel is installed, the next one can go on top and then slid over to the next position. The more panels installed, the more work room is available.

To minimize hazards of walking and carrying panels on the roof, the decision was made to move the scaffold to other positions (twice) around the yurt. You may not have that option. Use slats of wood to slide the panel across the roof. Make sure it is always held onto to prevent sliding off.

I'm holding the handle at the top of the panel, securing it from moving or slipping while the team slides the bottom edge and moves it about, making adjustments.

The bottom edge of the panel should be flush with the top edge of the beam. Center the panel between the beams' centerlines.

Once the panel is even on both rafters, a team member hammers in a spike.

Last panel! The entire installation only took two hours, including time to move scaffolding.

The next step for me is to tweek a couple of panels then insulate between them and cover with ice and snow shield.

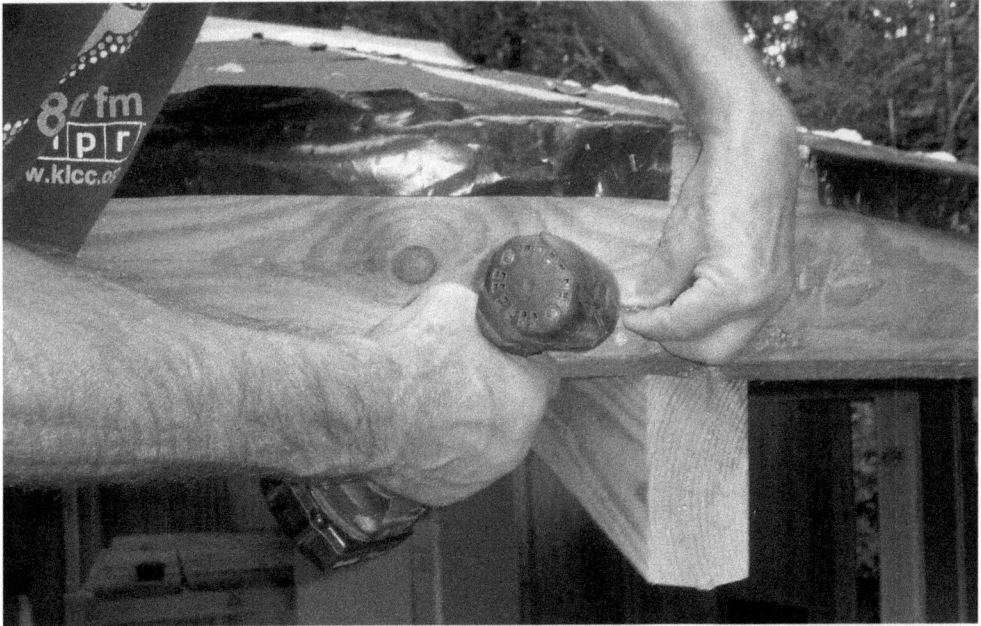

Two of the roof panels needed a trim to fit tight against the ring. The ring is not a perfect dodecagon, even though I tried. If you have the same issue. just secure the panel to the adjacent one with straps. Remove all the screws and spikes.

Lift up the panel, set it on a support, trim it to fit, then refasten it. I fastened a handle again to make the panel easier to move around and set back into place.

I marked and cut rigid foam insulation for the spaces between all the roof panels and the center ring.

A thin saw works, with the piece locked between two blocks on the table. The cut tended to venture, so I'd turn the piece over and cut for several inches, flip back over and cut the same length, and so on to the end.

155

I cut trim pieces and placed them at the ceiling peak against the ring and roof panel to prevent foam insulation from leaking in.

Short pieces of insulation were installed around the ring.

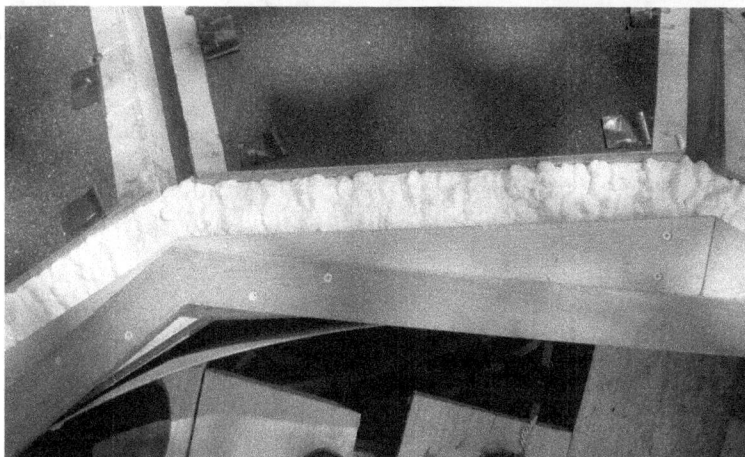

Spray foam insulation went in next, and once dry, trimmed off the top.

Before I started working out on the roof, I put on a harness that was securely fastened to the top of the tower. Working at the edge of a roof is dangerous work, so it's a good idea to take proper precautions.

Spray foam insulation goes in the bottom before adding the rigid foam, then on the sides and top to fill in any gaps.

The cut pieces fit pretty good for the most part, and I filled gaps and spaces with foam. When rain threatened before I was done, we covered up the seams with tarps until I could finish up and then add the ice and snow shield.

I cut strips of ice and snow shield to lay on all the hips (where two roof panels meet). I cut them long with plans to trim back from below once I installed the facsia and the drip edge. I then caulked all the hips to make sure they stay put until the final roofing goes up later.

The tops of the ice and snow shield strips were cut with a v-cut so they fit up to the ring framing.

After all the strips were down, I "flashed" over all of the roofing with a product called Forti-flashing®, which is a bituminous material with a flexible outer layer. It could be moulded into tight bends.

This will seal the upper roof completely from water intrusion. Later, it will still get a metal flashing overlay, which will protect the underlayer from sun damage.

I cut fascia from 1x fir material I had on hand. The fascia's purpose is to finish the roof panel ends and to cover up the gaps between the panels that you'd otherwise have to fill with something. It's not on the materials list because it's more of a finishing touch.

I ripped down my boards to just 3/8" wider than the roof panel thickness. If it was too wide, the bottom edge would collide with the rafter, making it stand too far out at its bottom of the roof panel.

The ends were pre-cut with a compound angle of 15° along the cut and a 5° angle from top to bottom of the board. The board's other end was left uncut. It would be measured and cut with the similar 15°/5° cut that would mate up to the next board put into place. The boards were also prefinished to save on ladder time.

As they were installed, the precut end mated up to a site cut end as I proceeded around the roof. Any miscuts or overlaps were taken care of by trimming off the over protruding tip of the fascia. All else was taken care of with a bit of caulk. Once the fascia was done, I installed a drip-edge flashing.

Even though I haven't made the roofing pieces yet, I wanted to have the flashing pieces made and in place for the winter. This is a little more complicated than the flashing for the 3-foot skylight as described earlier.

Because this skylight is an 8-sided unit and it sets on top of a 12-sided yurt, the flashing was convoluted. With eight points meeting twelve points, every other point would have to match up. If you draw two circles with the same diameter and divide one into twelve slices and the other into eight slices, you can overlay the two and see how this was accomplished.

That means that two pieces of flashing make up one leg of the 8-sided shape to account for the point that doesn't coincide.

At these junctions of flashing pieces I made them interlock. At the "matching" (8 in 12) points, the flashing simply overlapped. All of these joints would be caulked with a butyl caulk when the roof was finally placed and the flashings were installed one last time.

Installing the Skylight

Once you've finished the flashing, the skylight is ready to install. With a large skylight, it's mostly grunt work...and being careful! While this skylight dome is 6-feet diameter, the same process would be used for the 3-foot design. It will just be easier.

Whatever the dimensions of the skylight, you need a length of 3/4" wide foam with sticky face to place around the top of the opening framing. Once that's done, the skylight is fitted over the flashings, coming to rest on the foam tape.

Once the skylight is in place, four screws hold it down.

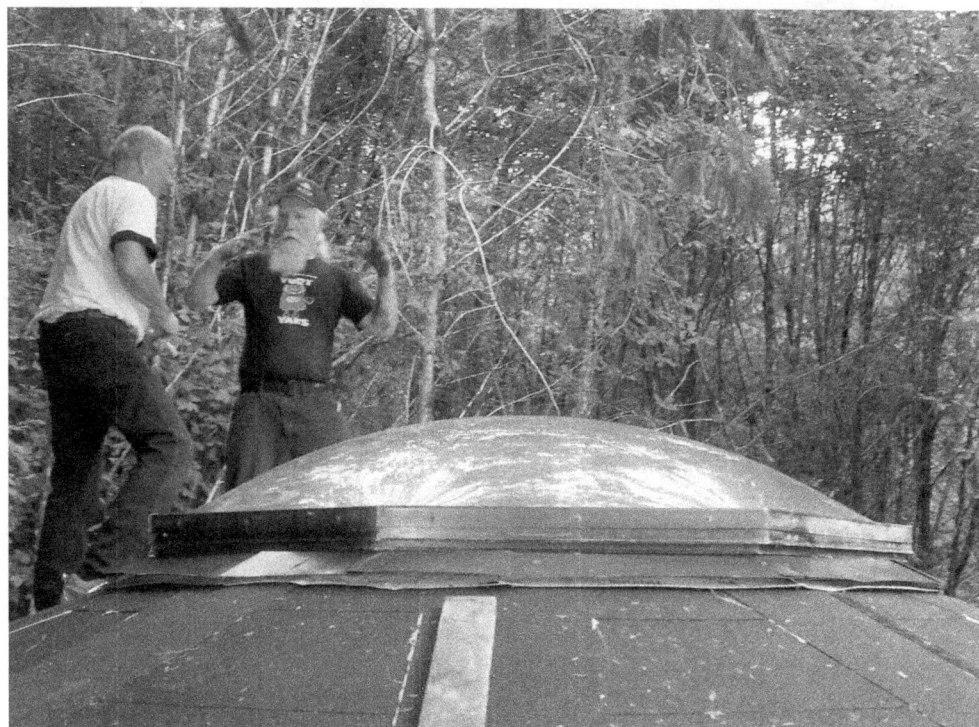

I'll wait for final roofing to get all installed permanently, but meanwhile, the dome is secure in case of high winds.

Final Bits

There was nothing left but details! I had metal strips of 26-gauge flashing cut at a roofing supplier. I custom-bent them with a 30° (or 150° leg to leg interior) angle to meet up with the house corners. They were also pre-drilled for easy application. Just a couple of screws were done for now until the corners inside are insulated.

As you can see, the windows were also installed around this time, which was just a matter of setting in the openings and screwing. I picked up the windows at a local wholesaler.

I decided to build a temporary set of steps with a deck planned for later. This is a quick and easy stair to make.

As with any stair, you start with the total rise from the landing (whatever that may be: ground, deck, porch) to the finish floor level the stair is to access. The next factor is the total run, or length the stair has to fit into or the desired length, determined by how deep you want the steps to be.

In this example, the total rise from the floor level to the ground at about four feet was 36 inches. This was very convenient for making five risers at 7-3/16" height. Now for the run. There is a guide in stair building that dictates that the sum of both rise and run should total about 18. That was making a 10" tread a very nice depth (a 2x10 fits between a 2x8 edges at this angle). These are open stairs, so there is no riser board to impede your foot as you walk up.

The layout is simple. Rough out the risers (the side pieces). Take a framing square and (using this stair as example) step off five times, marking the top of the treads as you go. For convenience, put tape on your framing square- with an arrow (up) at 7-3/16" (approximately) and at 10".

When accurately laid out on both stringers, go back and place a mark 1-1/2" below the layout mark for the bottom of the 2x tread.

Put a big pencil X below it to denote where to put the stair bracket. Now you can cut away the excess ends of the stringers. Keep in mind that you can either have a "step" at the level of the finish floor extending out, or the first step is "one down" as I did here. That will determine where you cut at the top. The bottom stays the same. Cut the steps/treads whatever your stair width will be minus the stringers. Place the stair brackets on both stringers on your X, aligning with the bottom of your tread line, or on the bottoms of the steps right at the outer edges.

A prefinish might be a good idea. Cut the bottom off with a level cut that coincides with the riser height from top of the tread to your cut-off line.

To assemble, begin by attaching the stringers to the structure outside of your floor level. This is probably a vertical surface (your stringer should have a vertical cut on it). Place so that the top of the first step out/down to finished floor level matches the riser height. Use a bracket to attach and appropriate screws or nails to hold it in place. Space them so that the interiors space/distance is the length you cut your treads to.

Squeeze the stringers together and nail or screw through the brackets that you mounted on either the treads or stringers. Make sure the top of your step/tread falls on the line you made as part of the layout of your stairs.

Once competely fastened, the stairs are ready for use.

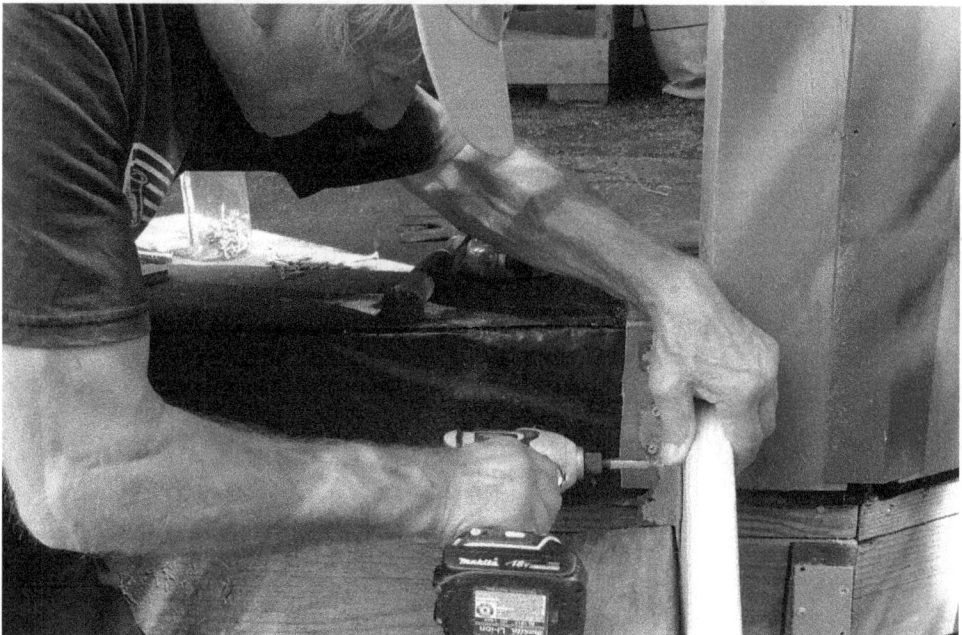

Robin found a 100+ year old door at a yard sale for $35. It is solid pine, no laminate. The interior just had a clear finish and the exterior had a few coats of paint. I sanded both sides, primed the exterior to be painted later, and cleaned up the old hardware. I had a jam saved from a remodel and used it to get the door installed.

I also added a drip edge. This will keep the water on the roof from running down the face of the fascia. Standard lengths come at 10 feet. The fascia is 5'-7" which would make for a lot of wasted metal. So, I cut a ten foot length in half and then installed a 12" piece at each of the twelve corners.

Cable cover blocking covers up the cables as viewed from the outside. They are similar to the wedge blocks in the interior with two ways to install them.

You can make the blocks parallel to the walls, or perpendicular to the top edge of the rafter.

The perpendicular way means the tops tip over at the 5° angle. Employ the 15° angle for the cheek cut against the rafter and the 5° tilt outward at the top. Cut one end and the other cut long or leave uncut. Get a dimension that fits the bottom edge of the block to just touch the wall sheathing. Two screws at each end holds the block in. Screws work nicely for this, with predrilled holes to ease fastening.

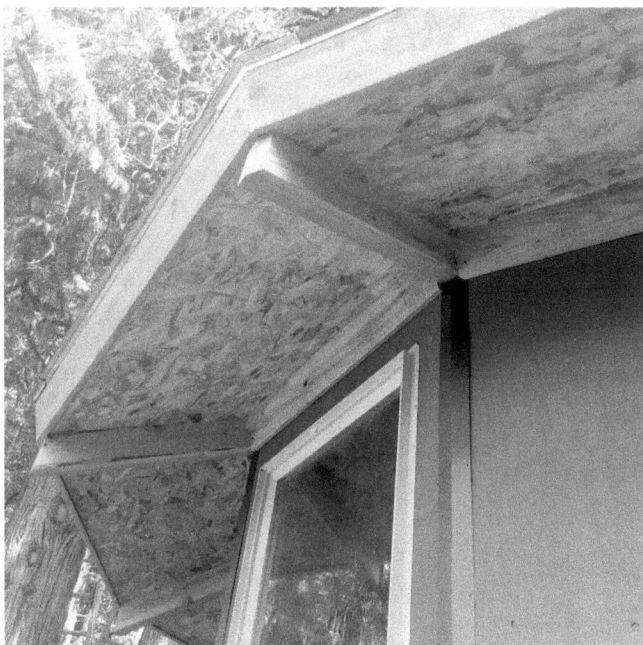

Install blocks after the cable cavity has been insulated (rigid or loose fill). Caulk the back side of the interior blocks at top, sides, bottom cracks first before you insulate.

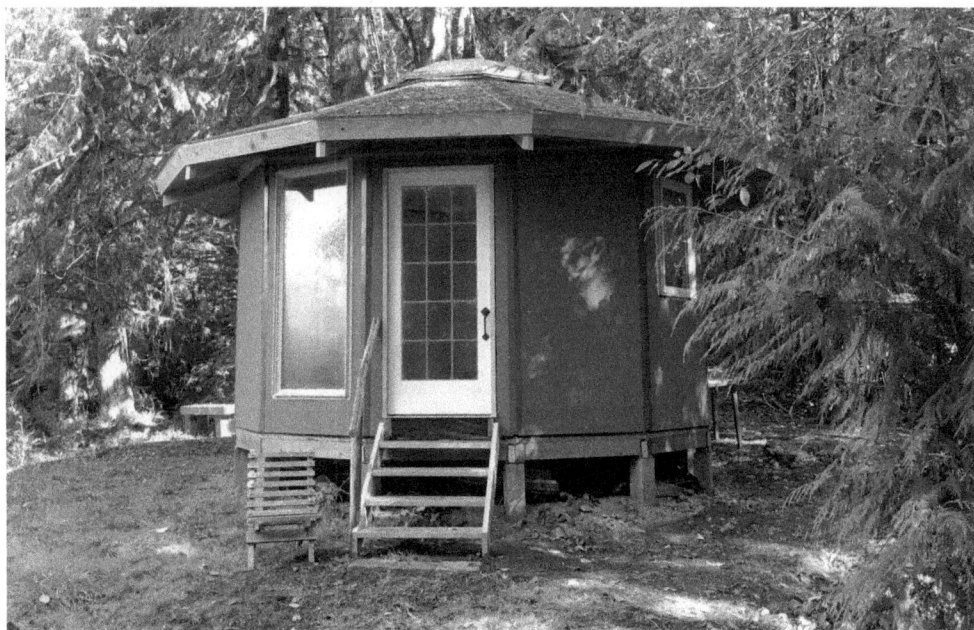

And it's done for now! This yurt will be a fun place to hang out this winter just as it stands. We'll finalize everything another time. The material list with costs are next, then some resources. Marvin has offered afterthoughts at the end.

YURT MATERIALS & COSTS

Here are almost all of the materials needed for this yurt along with prices in Lane County, Oregon in 2018. I may have left off a few minor things, but this is most of it. **Note that 2x4, 2x6, 4x4, and 4x6 do not denote dimensional measurements.**

FOUNDATION

QTY	MATERIAL	NOTES/SPECS	PRICE	TOTAL
12	Concrete pads	12x8x8 (footings)	2.99	36.00
02	8' 4x4 pressure treated post	cut to 16" (perimeter posts)	10.47	20.94
06	4-1/2"x1/2" bolts w/nut and washer	4" (footing to post)	2.61	15.66
04	12"x12" concrete pads	footings for center support	2.99	12.00
1	4x8 1/2" plywood	cut into 4-2'x'2 squares	42.99	42.99
1	8' 4x4 pressure treated	cut to 24" posts (4 corners of pad)	10.47	10.47
06	10' 4x6 pressure treated	cut to length (support beams)	20.97	125.82
12	Tie plates TP37	(tie beam to beam)	1.11	13.32
12	tie straps LSTA12	(tie post to beam)	.99	11.88
2	boxes TECO nails	(for plates and straps)		
		joist hanger nails #8x1-1/2"	2.63	5.38
12	8' 2x4 pressure treated	(cut for post bracing)	4.87	58.44
1	box 3"x#9 coated screws	box 350 ct @30.99 need 75 ct.	9.99	9.99
1	box 2"x#9 coated screws	box 350 ct @24.99 need 75 ct.	8.49	8.49
1	box 1# 16d 3-1/2" galvanized nails		4.99	4.99
1#	8d 2-1/2" galvanized nails	approx. 92 ct. in 1/2#	4.99	4.99

FLOOR SYSTEM

QTY	MATERIAL	NOTES/SPECS	PRICE	TOTAL
6	10' 2x8 pressure treated	(perimeter framing)	12.97	77.82
36	8' 2x8 pressure treated	(interior framing)	10.97	394.92
7#	8d 2-1/2" (about 650)	(6" nail pattern)	4.99	34.93
12	4x8 sheets 3/4" CDX plywood	(sheathing)	33.98	407.76
24	sheets 2" rigid insulation	(optional) with foil	34.99	839.76
OR				
4	bags R-21 insulation	(optional)	57.99	231.96
1	50' 48" hardware cloth 1/4x1/4	(optional for insulation protection)	3.89/ft.	194.50
2#	3/4" galvanized fence staples	(if hardware cloth is used)	3.19/lb.	6.39

WALLS

QTY	MATERIAL	NOTES/SPECS	PRICE	TOTAL
12	10' 2x4 standard/better	(top/bottom plates)	4.99	59.88
50	8' 2x4 standard/better	(36 studs +2 ea for ea. Door/window, etc.)	3.99	199.50
12	4x8 1/2" CDX plywood	(sheathing)	23.95	287.40
12	strap ties LSTA18	(wall to beams)	1.59	19.08
1	12' 4x4 pressure treated post	ripped for 12 wall wedges x2 (1 ft. length)	17.27	17.27
2	boxes 3"x9# coated screws	(through framing into wall wedges)	9.99	19.98
1	box TECO nails	(strap nailing)	2.69	2.69
1	box #8x1-1/4" screws	(strap nailing)	9.49	9.49
3-1/2#	3-1/2" 16d galvanized nails	(nailing of framing)	4.99	17.46
16#	2-1/2" 8d galvanized nails	(nailing of sheathing)	4.99	79.84

CABLES

QTY	MATERIAL	NOTES/SPECS	PRICE	TOTAL
2	52' 3/8" galvanized aircraft cable	one end waged with thimble eye		100.00
	thimbles	(1 each cable, to make eye)	tbd	
6	cable clamps	(3 each cable)	tbd	

BEAMS/RAFTERS

QTY	MATERIAL	NOTES/SPECS	PRICE	TOTAL
12	10' 4x6 #2/6tr Douglas fir	(or equivalent – pick out nice ones as they will be visible)	18.99	227.88
1	10'x1/2" electric conduit	(cut 12 3-1/2" sleeves for cable through rafter beam)	2.75	2.75
12	3/8"x11" galvanized bolts	with nut & washer +extra washers for spacers if needed	1.83	21.97
1	¼"x12" drill bit	(pilot holes)	8.27	8.27
1	3/8"x12" drill bit	(bolt holes)	12.47	12.47
48	12' 2x6 std/btr Douglas fir	(blocking between beam/rafters @ wall interior both inside & outside	7.69	61.52
24	A23 angle brackets	(ties rafters to top plate wall)	.88	21.12

ROOF PANELS

QTY	MATERIAL	NOTES/SPECS	PRICE	TOTAL
12	4x8 1/2" CDX plywood	(sheathing main area of roof panel)	23.95	287.40
OR				
12	4x8 1/2" OSB	(sheathing main area of roof panel)	17.55	210.60
60	10' 2x4 std/btr Douglas fir	(or equivalent, framing members)	4.99	299.40
16	2" sheets rigid insulation	(optional) (2 layers)	28.99	463.84
10#	8d galvanized nails	(6" nail pattern) about 1000 nails	4.99	49.90
10#	2" 16d galvanized nails	(framing connection – 3 each connection	4.99	49.90
120	8" gutter spikes	(ties roof panels to beam rafters)	.49	58.80
48	8"x3/16" hex drive screws	(ties @top and bottom of panel)	1.50	72.00
6	12' 1x6 fascia (primed SPF)	(finish fascia board)	11.39	68.34
1-1/2#	8d galvanized finish nails	(for nailing fascia)	2.79	4.19

SKYLIGHT RING

QTY	MATERIAL	NOTES/SPECS	PRICE	TOTAL
1	12' 2x12 std/btr Douglas fir	(one clean edge and face) 19.49	19.49	
1	12' 2x4 std/btr Douglas fir	(or equivalent)	6.29	6.29
1/2	4x8 CDX plywood	(cut into pieces, glued to 2x12 + 2x4)	23.95	23.95
1	8 oz bottle glue	exterior wood glue	6.00-11.00	11.00
1	10'x14" 12g metal	(interior ring)	68.00	68.00
12	1-1/2"x#10 coated screws	(screw metal to wood ring)		
2	10' 2"x3" flashing	(top cap) 90° angle	8.99	17.98
2	10' roll 1/4" thick x 3/4" wide	foam tape	3.49	6.98

SKYLIGHT ASSEMBLY

QTY	MATERIAL	NOTES/SPECS	PRICE	TOTAL
1	36" skylight with 6" rise		296.00	296.00
1	8' 2x6 pressure treated	(base) ripped deck board	6.57	6.57
2	10' 2"x2" flashing	90° angle	7.99	15.98
1	10' roll 1/4" thick x 3/4" wide	foam tape	3.49	3.49
1	12' 1-1/2"x1-1/2"x1/8"	aluminum angle metal	16.00	16.00
16'	6" butyl flashing	or other flexible flashing t i.e. FortiFlash	.79	12.64

TOWER

QTY	MATERIAL	NOTES/SPECS	PRICE	TOTAL
12	10' 2x4 std/btr Douglas fir	(to build the tower)	4.99	59.88
1	box 3"x#10 coated screws		9.99	9.99

MATERIALS APPROXIMATE TOTAL: $5,500

Resources

Videos

Here are the links to videos showing Marvin constructing the floor panels, roof panels, and rafters for this yurt:

Building a Wood-Framed Panelized Yurt: the Floor Panels: https://youtu.be/2K8GrLSXceE

Building a Wood-Framed Panelized Yurt: the Roof Panels: https://youtu.be/Qp-FqUSf58jA

Building a Wood-Framed Panelized Yurt: the Rafters: https://youtu.be/c_S_1I2p2k0

Yurt Companies

If you prefer to skip building the yurt components, there are companies out there that do it for you. You will have, shipped to your site, a "ready to assemble" yurt with instructions and professional advice. In alphabetical order, these companies sell the parts for frame panel yurts:

California Yurts: www.yurtpeople.com
Deltec Homes: www.deltechomes.com
Goulburn Yurtworks: www.yurtworks.com.au
Mandala Custom Homes: www.mandalahomes.com
Round Foot Homes: www.roundfoothomes.com
Smiling Woods Yurts: www.smilingwoodsyurts.com

If you are interested in a fabric yurt, a number of companies that sell those components are listed on yurtinfo.org

You can purchase a complete skylight dome here:
Tam Skylights: www.tamskylights.com
Or, just the skylight:
Multicraft Plastics: www.multicraftplastics.com/

Plans for a tapered wall yurt: www.yurtinfo.org/the-yurt-foundation

---

Credits

All photos are by Robin Koontz and Marvin Denmark with these exceptions: **Keith Grossman**: 152, 153; **iStockPhoto:** Sebastien Durand: 8-9; Lucy Brown: 10; Serjopak: 12-13; Cindy Chow: 14; Coprid: 15; Lannomadav: 15; Ozbalci: 16-17

YurtYaks logo and drawings by Marvin Denmark

Random Thoughts on Yurts

My interest in construction or making things in general probably had its start when I was very young. We had just moved to another farm several miles from our previous farm, when I turned six. Shortly after moving, my father along with his father, my two older brothers and an uncle (on occasions) built a 40' X 60' pole barn. To my knowledge none of them had any real construction experience. My dad was a butcher, my granddad worked at a flour mill, although on the side he had a business of repairing furniture (he had a fun shop), and my uncle worked in electrical matters. But they got it built and it was fun to play in….not so much to work in. For me making things followed from then on.

During the first or second grade, probably during the summer break, I carved a "bowie" knife out of wood. As any good elementary school student I had to take it to school to show it off. It was probably hard to keep concealed. In any case my teacher took it away from me and promised I'd get it back at the end of the school year. I never did. But I went on to carve others, as well as six-shooters of wood. My crowning achievement was a boat, more of a trough, that I built to ride around in our cattle pond. When I and my youngest sister got in to try it out, it promptly sank. I didn't take into account water weight displacement.

My first interest in yurts came through a picture. Sometime around 1979 or 80, I was reading a magazine. I don't recall the article but the photograph struck me. It was taken looking up through the skylight with the rafters radiating out all around, like the depiction of the sun with large rays shooting out. It probably had 24-28 rafters around. I loved it. I cut the photograph out and saved it. It was in my files for many years but sometime must have been lost. When I got a job contracting the construction of a house composed of three yurts with connectors I recalled that image. And when the project was done I could see the same image in reality, 28 rafters radiating out from the large skylight.

The size of a small yurt is the function of several factors. If it is too small it loses it's shape as and appeal of a yurt. As it gets larger it simply becomes a house, not that that is bad. I can't say what is a good size as cutoff. At present I am working out the details for building a 20' diameter yurt. I think that still qualifies for small.

I said several factors above. Another one is the width of the wall segments. The reason that this is important is that wall segments define the panelized yurt. And in designing a yurt the wall is roughly 4' wide. Why four feet? That is the width of a standard sheet of plywood. And, that width allows ample room for a large window or a three foot entry door to be placed within. But don't get hung up on the 4' dimension exactly. I'll show you what I mean.

Looking at this 16' yurt we'll apply the 4' segment rule (I'll call it that). If you remember, circumference is equal to diameter times pi : C = 16' X 3.1416 = 50.26' If we use the "rule", then 50.26 divided by 4 = 12.56. Not a particularly good rafter layout. So you go back and divide 50.26 by 12 (now that's a good rafter layout) and you get 4'- 2. 1/4". That's still not the correct number since it is an arc dimension and you need the chord length dimension. There is a formula (chord length) for that but I'll skip it and just tell you that I used trigonometry. You know two things: the hypotenuse (8' the radius (16'/2)) and the angle 15 degrees [30 degrees = (360 / 12) but you need a right triangle - one with a 90 degree angle in it, thus 30 / 2 gives you 15.

Did I lose you? Good. Now think of a 16" pizza pie. Cut it in half. Now cut both of those in half. Now cut each of those into thirds. You just made a pizza of 12 slices 8" on the side. And you'll say "but where is the trig"? Take one of your slices and nibble off the crust so that there is a straight line from corner to corner, and then fold it in half. You just made what I described above. But you don't need trigonometry. If you had laid out your pizza and cut it very accurately, you could measure the bottom length and it would come out just over 4". In my calculations above the segment is 49. 11/16 " long [the right triangle segment (the folded slice) was 24.846", then times 2 = 49.693]. So you could do this all just by drawing it out accurately.

Look mom, no math!

That takes me to my next topic. Working accurately. You can do anything and everything in three ways: the wrong way twice, wrong once and the second to correct it or do it right the first time. I always like to ask: "If you don't have the time to do it right the first time, when will you have time to do it over if you did it wrong?" Accuracy could be defined several different ways, but what I'm thinking about here has more to do with your mind, which effects your accuracy. Are you paying attention to what you are doing? Anyone can cut a board; they could also cut a hand off. Are your hands doing one thing and your thinking going some other direction. You can only do one thing at a time. At best you may be able to switch very quickly between two different things but you are still only doing effectively one thing. So when you are doing any one of the tasks in this book put yourself completely in the process of whatever you are undertaking. You'll be more accurate and you won't be letting in all of those negative thoughts from elsewhere. The time to daydream and let your mind wonder is in thinking about building this yurt and what you want to do with it....and those are fun thoughts.

Working accurately and paying attention leads me to another thought: Working with your hands. It doesn't seem to get a good report now. People don't want to be known as someone who works with their hands. It is perceived as manual labor, and that is true. Because it is manual, but it may not just be labor. If you read the above and I assume you did, you know it engages the mind. And unless the labor is forced upon you, it can be enjoyable. The connection between the hands doing something and the engaged mind is fun. In fact, it is play. And that is what all of your "work" should be.

Recycling seems like such a no-brainer in building a small yurt project. Everywhere I could I used something that had had a previous use, whether it was the footings or the used deck beams. Later, the skylight used was recycled from a previous job that I had done. The windows were purchased from a company that specializes in buying mis-manufactured products, maybe with very minor flaws. As long as the substitute doesn't impact the structural integrity of the building it seems a natural to use something that still has a "life" and can maybe add something special the project.

Finally, I think this small yurt can be scaled to several different slightly larger sizes. I am currently working on all of the details for a 20' diameter yurt. Those details will be posted to the YurtYaks site when I complete them. I am exploring the possibilities for various other "small" sizes. That too when completed will be posted to the site. Meanwhile, happy building! I hope you have fun building this yurt. If you have improvements or come up with innovative solutions to problems in construction please inform us and other readers. We can all learn more.

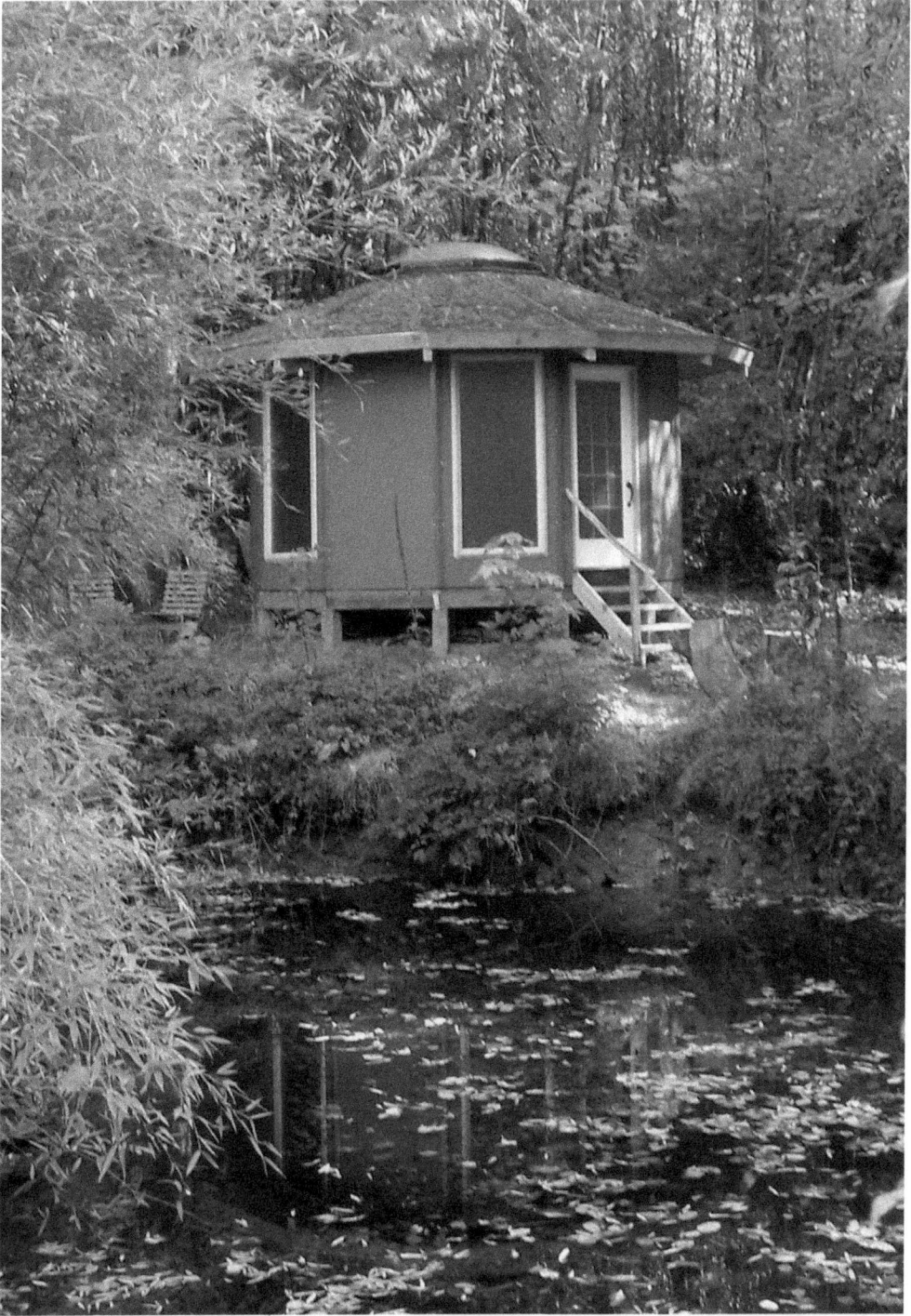

For updates and more information and discussion about building a wood-framed panelized yurt, join our Facebook page: facebook.com/yurtyaks/

www.ingramcontent.com/pod-product-compliance
Lightning Source LLC
Chambersburg PA
CBHW080530090426
42733CB00015B/2540